For reference

Not to be taken from the room.

TEXAS LAW

In Layman's Language

Lone Star Books®
An imprint of Gulf Publishing Company
Houston, Texas

TEXAS LAW

In Layman's Language

SIXTH EDITION

Charles Turner
Ralph Walton

TEXAS LAW
In Layman's Language

Published by Lone Star Books
An Imprint of the Rowman & Littlefield Publishing Group
4720 Boston Way
Lanham, Maryland 20706

Distributed by National Book Network

Library of Congress Cataloging-in-Publication Data

Turner, Charles, 1936–
     Texas law in layman's language / Charles Turner and Ralph Walton. — 6th ed.
          p.   cm.
     Includes index.
     ISBN 0-88415-489-0 (alk. paper)
     1. Law—Texas—Popular works.   I. Walton, Ralph, 1897–1990.   II. Title.
     KFT1281.W3   1999
     349.764—dc21   99-31400
                                                                     CIP

Printed in the United States of America.

Printed on acid-free paper (∞).

Contents

Preface, vi
Introduction, viii

Preface

Texas Law in Layman's Language was originally published in 1970, with subsequent editions in 1975, 1983, 1990, and 1995. The legislature continues to pass new statutes and the courts continue to reinterpret old ones; growth and evolution is an inherent part of the legal system—so another edition is necessary.

The goal of this edition remains the same: to provide Texas citizens with a concise, understandable book that discusses laws that most affect their daily lives. Law is a complex subject, however, and the choice of subjects is highly selective. Many important areas could not be included and, additionally, this book deals with general principles. It is no substitute for consultation with a competent attorney when facing a specific legal problem.

The text begins with a discussion of family law, since most litigation today involves divorce and other family matters that impact the lives of many citizens. There are also chapters dealing with wills, estates, probate, and property—all of which are areas of obvious importance to most people. There is a section, too, that discusses the landlord-tenant relationship. This is an especially important area for urban apartment dwellers.

Many people are involved in various business relationships, such as partnerships, limited partnerships, and corporations, without understanding the meaning of those relationships. They may become partners without realizing the relationship exists. Everyone should be aware of worker's compensation insurance, arbitration of disputes, mediation, the statute of limitations for personal actions, and similar subjects that can directly affect one's personal life, as well as business relationships. This book includes a section discussing Texas consumer protection statutes. An entire chapter is also devoted to the employer-employee relationship—an area of increasing litigation.

Every citizen should know what to do when sued, so there is a section on civil procedure, as well. A chapter dealing with the Texas Penal Code and the Code of Criminal Procedure is also important; while most citizens do not intend to run afoul of the criminal law, it still happens frequently. An understanding of the way the system works can be of considerable value.

I hope this book will be pleasant reading for ordinary people and that it will bring a better understanding of the laws that govern daily life. I also hope that it will appeal to students, especially those who are thinking about law as a career.

Ralph Walton, the original sole author of this volume, passed away in 1990. This revised edition is dedicated to his memory.

Charles Turner

Introduction

What Is Law?

What is law? Most of us think the answer to that question is obvious. But legal scholars struggle to define this simple word. It is obvious that law consists of the rules enforced by society on its individual members. This definition, however, is clearly inadequate, for law is also a primary tool in reconciling competing interests and resolving conflicts within society. Courts and legislatures struggle to define the difference between law, custom, and morality (though rarely described in these terms), and to decide what the law ought to be and what it should accomplish.

Sources of Law

From where does law come? A philosophical answer to that question is beyond the scope of this book. Practically speaking, however, we can look at several sources of law in our system.

Constitutional Law

The highest level of law in our nation is that based on the United States Constitution; any federal or state law that is contrary to the Constitution will eventually be set aside. Our Constitution is broadly written, which makes it subject to considerable latitudes of interpretation. This interpretative role is uniquely the function of the United States Supreme Court. However strongly we might feel that a particular interpretation is wrong, we are nevertheless bound by that decision; it is the law of the land unless modified or overturned by a later Supreme Court decision, or by a constitutional amendment.

Most states also have constitutions, as does Texas, and these constitutions occupy a similar primacy as to state law. The Texas Constitution has been the subject of criticism because, unlike the federal document, it is written in great detail, requiring an unending flow of proposed amendments to be submitted to the voters. An attempt to write a new constitution for the state was rejected by the voters of Texas in 1975.

Statutory Law

A second source of law is legislative—at the national level, this involves laws passed by Congress; at the state level, statutes enacted by legislatures; and, at the local level, municipal ordinances enacted by city council members. Subject to their constitutionality, these laws are binding on the courts, although courts have the significant role of interpretation. For example, in the Texas Tort Claims Act, the legislature provided for situations in which various governmental institutions are liable for the negligence of their employees, thereby partially rejecting the old common law doctrine of governmental immunity. Subsequently, by its interpretation of the statute, the Texas Supreme Court actually increased the potential liability of governmental institutions beyond what appeared to be the obvious meaning of the statute. So, though statutes are a source of law, one must remember that courts officially interpret the meaning and application of statutes to particular situations.

Common Law

A third source of law is the common law, or judge-made law. Originally, this was the source of most law in our nation. It is the law written by courts on a case-by-case basis, arising out of specific situations. Its hallmark is the concept of *stare decisis,* that is, that courts should follow the precedents of prior decisions. The common law developed in England and its principles have evolved over centuries. In this country, we are increasingly moving away from common law toward codifications of law. Yet the common law is still the source of much of our jurisprudence, such as torts, contracts, property, and evidence.

Administrative Law

The most rapidly growing area of law today consists of the rules and hearings of administrative agencies. More and more legislative bodies are creating agencies and delegating rule-making authority to them. It is difficult even for practicing attorneys to keep up with the flow of regulations from this source. Texas alone has more than 75 licensing and regulatory agencies. Statistics indicate that in 1977, legislative bodies at the federal, state, and local levels enacted approximately 150,000 new laws, and each of these laws, on the average, required the issuance of 10 new regulations.

How Effective Is Our Legal System?

The effectiveness of our legal system is being questioned now as never before. Legal scholars point out that the United States has three times the number of lawyers as England and 20 times as many as Japan. In the 15 years before 1978, the number of lawyers increased by more than 50 percent, from 300,000 to 460,000. Legal fees have now climbed to more than $25 billion per year.

The increase in litigation in recent years has been overwhelming. Yet, with all this involvement in our legal system, the evidence mounts that the system fails to provide justice for large numbers of people. Even at its peak, it is estimated that the federal Legal Services Corporation, handling a million cases annually, met less than 15 percent of the need for legal services among the poor. And this does not account for the many lower-middle-class people who do not qualify for legal aid, yet do not have the resources to hire private attorneys. Lawrence Tribe, a professor of law at Harvard University, summarizes it well: "Too much law, too little justice; too many rules, too few results—that is our problem."

These problems are already engaging the attention of legal scholars, legislators, and the organized bar. It is, however, important for lay people to be aware of the situation and of possible solutions. For, ultimately, changes in our legal system must come from the people.

1. The Law and the Family

Family legal problems impact the lives of more people than any other area of law, with the possible exception of traffic violations. This chapter looks at some of the most important principles of law that affect families.

Husband and Wife

Celebration of Marriage

Marriage ceremonies may be performed by ordained ministers and priests; Jewish rabbis; authorized officers of religious organizations; justices of the peace; and judges of any courts of the state, including federal judges and excepting judges of municipal courts.

Who Shall Not Marry

Unless authority has been granted by court order, persons under 14 years of age are forbidden to marry.

License

The law requires persons who want to marry to obtain a marriage license from the county clerk, which is directed to all authorized persons to perform the marriage ceremony and is sufficient authority to perform the marriage.

Both the man and woman must appear before the county clerk and submit proof of their identity and age. They must also sign a statement as to whether an applicant is delinquent in the payment of court-ordered child support. The clerk, however, cannot use a person's response as a reason to refuse a license. It is not necessary that the license be issued in the county where the couple resides. In addition, a license must not be issued if either applicant has been divorced from another person within the past 30 days, unless by authority of a court order.

An unmarried male, 18 years of age or older, and an unmarried female, 18 years of age or older, who are not otherwise disqualified may contract and consent to marriage. Those individuals younger than 18 are not authorized to marry without the parents' or guardians' consent. If a minor does not have a parent or guardian, or if they refuse to consent, the county clerk is forbidden to issue a marriage license unless the couple obtains a court order.

A person who is under 18 years of age may petition in his or her own name in a district court for an order granting permission to marry. The petition must include a statement of the reasons the minor desires to marry. The court will appoint a guardian to represent the minor. If the judge believes it is in the best interest of the parties, he may advance the hearing on the docket so that an early hearing is obtained. The case will be heard by the judge without a jury based on what he believes to be in the best interest of the parties.

Normally the marriage cannot be performed during a 72-hour period immediately following the issuance of the marriage license, unless one of the parties is a member of the armed forces on active duty. A marriage license expires 30 days after it is issued. A minister or judge who performs a ceremony after that time commits a misdemeanor. A person authorized to perform marriage ceremonies is prohibited from discriminating against applicants on the basis of race, religion, or national origin.

Void Marriages

The law forbids marriages within certain close kinships by blood and provides a two- to ten-year penitentiary sentence for violation. A person may not marry:

1. An ancestor or descendant, by blood or adoption.
2. A brother or sister, of whole or half-blood relation, or by adoption.
3. A parent's brother or sister, of whole or half-blood relation.
4. A son or daughter of a brother or sister, of whole or half-blood relation, or by adoption.

A marriage entered into in violation of these provisions is void.

A marriage is void if either party was previously married and the prior marriage was not dissolved. However, the marriage becomes valid when the prior marriage is dissolved if since the dissolution of the prior marriage the parties have lived together as husband and wife and represented themselves to others as being married.

A marriage that is void is not a marriage at all. Other marriages are said to be "voidable." These are marriages subject to being set aside or annulled for some reason, such as the age of the parties. If not challenged, the marriage is legal.

Same-Sex Marriages

Clerks may not issue a license for the marriage of persons of the same sex. Only a man and a woman can get married in Texas.

Marriage Contracts

The law considers a marriage relationship as a partnership, but sometimes persons intending to marry want a premarital contract in order to have the separate rights of one or both of them established. On January 1, 1968, married women were fully emancipated. Married women can now transfer the title or mortgage of their separate property or the part of the community property they control and manage, without their husband's agreement. Women can make binding agreements with their husbands regarding separate and community property, a privilege they did not have before. Such premarital contracts are not important to most young couples, but they can be of great importance to older couples with established estates.

In 1987, Texas passed the Uniform Premarital Agreement Act, which recognizes the validity of a premarital agreement if it is in writing and signed by both parties. This statute gives broad authority to the parties to categorize their respective rights in particular items of property. They can even provide for the disposition of their property in the event of separation or divorce. Until recently, such agreements would have been unconstitutional. However, in November 1985, Section 15 of Article XVI of the Texas Constitution was amended to authorize spouses to determine which of their property would be separate and which would be community—not only existing property, but property to be acquired in the future. Parties entering a marriage now have great flexibility in deciding how their property is to be classified.

Contracts defining property rights between the husband and wife with respect to land (real property) and its attachment should be recorded in the county clerk's office in the county or counties where the property is located.

Personal or movable property is often transferred across county lines within the state, and any contracts dealing with the interest in or right of each spouse to that property should be recorded in the secretary of state's office in Austin, which is now the only place where personal property contracts are kept.

The wife's separate acknowledgment on a contract, deed, or mortgage is no longer required by law. Her acknowledgment form and a notary public's certification evidencing her acknowledgment are now the same as her husband's or any unmarried person's.

Duty to Support

Section 2.501 of the Family Code provides that each spouse has the duty to support the other spouse, and each parent has the duty to support his or her minor child. A spouse or parent who fails to discharge this duty is liable to anyone who provides "necessaries" to the spouse or child. Under the old statute, the wife was obligated to support her husband only when he was unable to support himself. That condition has now been removed, and the husband and wife have equal obligations toward one another.

If a wife goes to the grocery store and buys groceries for herself and the children, because these are necessities, the husband shares the liability for paying the bills. The same is true of the wife if the husband makes the purchases. If a suit is brought and judgment is taken under these circumstances, the court can direct what property will be sold first to pay the indebtedness and what will be sold next out of the several classes of property that the spouses own.

The Common Law Marriage

Despite all the provisions of the statutes, if a man and a woman agree to be married, live together as husband and wife, and publicly present themselves as man and wife without obtaining a marriage license and going through a legal marriage ceremony, they nevertheless are considered in law to be husband and wife. Their children are legitimate and capable of inheriting from the father as well as from the mother, just as if the parents had complied with all of the law's requirements for a legal marriage. In 1989, the legislature provided that in the event the parties to an informal marriage permanently separate, suit to establish the validity of the marriage must be brought within one year of the separation. Otherwise, the marriage ceases to be legally recognized. This gets close to common law divorce.

The husband and wife in a common law marriage have the same rights under the homestead law and the same exemptions from forced sale as those who comply with the formalities and consummate a legal marriage. There is now a provision in the law for registration of a common law marriage in the county of the couple's residence. This is done by executing a "declaration and registration of informal marriage" form that can be obtained in the county clerk's office. If the parties are underage, there must be attached an acknowledged consent executed by a parent of each underage person. The declaration is then recorded by the county clerk, and is then *prima facie* evidence of the marriage of the parties. A common law marriage, however, can exist without this declaration. The declaration just makes it easier to prove.

Agreements in Contemplation of Nonmarital Cohabitation

Traditionally, Texas has not looked favorably on nonmarital cohabitation and has been reluctant to lend judicial support to clarifying property rights involved in these relationships. This is changing, however, as mores change and such arrangements gain increased social acceptance. The well-known *Marvin* case in California sounded the alert that parties who cohabit without marriage may nevertheless acquire property rights.

In 1987, Texas passed S. B. 281, "An Act Restricting the Use of Palimony Suits," which amended the statute of frauds to require that "an agreement made on consideration of nonmarital conjugal cohabitation" must be in writing to be enforceable. While this statute certainly prohibits any claim based on oral contracts, it sanctions written agreements and grants a certain legislative recognition of the relationship. It probably does not inhibit other existing judicial theories based on partnership and trusts. Many unanswered questions remain, however.

Dissolution of the Marriage by Annulment or Divorce

Annulment

It is presumed each party to a marriage is potent and without other impediment that would render the marriage void. In a case where one of the spouses finds the other has such a disability, then the marriage relation can be dissolved or annulled by a suit in a district court. The suit alleges that the disability existed before the marriage and that the fact was unknown to the plaintiff (the one bringing the suit) at the time of the marriage.

The cause for annulment must exist at the time of marriage: Annulment is based upon the assumption that there never was a valid marriage, and, therefore, it should be declared void. One induced to marry by false representation of material facts has the right of annulment, and marriages may be dissolved on proof of fraud, duress, or mental incapacity of one or the other party. Irregularities in the marriage license application, the lack of proper witnesses, or other technical deficiencies are not causes for annulment.

Persons under 18 years of age are required by law to obtain their parents' consent to marry if the parents are living. If one parent is dead, then the consent of the survivor is needed. If both parents are dead and there is a guardian, his consent must be obtained.

If persons under 18 years of age marry (either formally or informally) without the proper consent or court order, the marriage is subject to annulment. Such an annulment proceeding can be filed by the parent, guardian, managing conservator or "best friend" of the minor, provided the suit is filed within 90 days after the petitioner knew or should have known about the marriage, or within 90 days after the 14th birthday of the underage party. If not brought within this time, it is barred. In no case can such a suit be brought after the underage person has reached 18 years of age. The decision to annul the marriage is within the discretion of the judge. As a practical matter, it is unlikely that courts will set aside marriages of older teenagers—and certainly not if the wife is pregnant.

Divorce

A suit for divorce presumes a marriage is valid but asks that the relationship be dissolved for post-nuptial causes. Section 6.001, f.f. of the Texas Family Code sets out the following seven grounds for divorce:

1. *Insupportability.* This is the Texas "no-fault" provision. Today most divorces are granted on this basis. On the petition of either party, a divorce may be granted without regard to fault if the "marriage has become insupportable because of discord or conflict of personalities that destroys the legitimate ends of the marriage relationship and prevents any reasonable expectation of reconciliation." Frequently, this is the basis of a divorce even when other grounds are present, because a no-fault approach is more likely to reduce the anger of the parties and bring about a reasonable settlement of other issues.
2. *Cruelty.* A divorce may be granted in favor of one spouse if the other spouse is guilty of cruel treatment toward the complaining spouse that renders further living together insupportable.
3. *Adultery.* A divorce may be decreed in favor of one spouse if the other spouse has committed adultery. Proof of adultery, however, must be based on clear and positive evidence, not on mere suggestion and innuendo.

4. *Conviction of a felony.* A divorce may be decreed in favor of one spouse if since the marriage the other spouse (a) has been convicted of a felony; (b) has been imprisoned for at least one year in the state penitentiary, a federal penitentiary, or the penitentiary of another state; and (c) has not been pardoned. A divorce may not be granted under this section against a spouse who was convicted on the testimony of the other spouse.

5. *Abandonment.* A divorce may be decreed in favor of one spouse if the other spouse left the complaining spouse with the intention of abandonment and remained away at least one year.

6. *Living apart.* A divorce may be decreed in favor of either spouse if the spouses have lived apart without cohabitation for at least three years.

7. *Confinement in a mental hospital.* A divorce may be decreed in favor of one spouse if at the time the suit is filed (a) the other spouse has been confined in a mental hospital as defined in the Texas Mental Health Code in this state or in another state for at least three years, and (b) it appears that the spouse's mental disorder is of such a degree and nature that he is not likely to adjust, or that if he adjusts, it is probable that he will suffer a relapse.

These are the only grounds provided by Texas law for divorce. The spouse bringing suit for divorce may allege one or more of these grounds in the petition, but only one ground is sufficient if proved satisfactorily in court.

Time Element in Divorce Suits

One who brings a suit for divorce in this state must have been a bona fide resident of the state of Texas for six months and of the county in which the suit is brought for the 90 days preceding the filing of the suit. A trial cannot be held until 60 days have expired from the date the suit was filed.

Testimony of the Husband or Wife

In divorce suits and proceedings, the husband and wife may testify against each other. However, a divorce will not be granted if there is collusion between them.

Debts Created after Suit

Formerly the husband had management, control, and disposition of the general community property during marriage. Now, under Section 3.102 of the Family Code, each spouse has the sole management, control, and disposition of the community property he or she would have owned if single, including, among other things, personal earnings, revenue from separate property and revenues from personal injuries.

Unless otherwise provided in writing, general community property is to be under the joint management and control of the husband and wife. Nevertheless, after a petition for divorce is filed and until a final decree is entered, a transfer of real or personal community property is void with respect to the other spouse, if the transfer was made with the intent to injure the rights of the other spouse. This is not true, however, if the party dealing with the wrongdoing spouse had no notice of the intent to injure the other spouse.

While a divorce suit is pending, both husband and wife have the right to request that an inventory of the property in the other's possession be made. In addition, either party may obtain an injunction restraining the other from disposing of any community property under his or her control.

Temporary Relief

When a divorce action is filed it is often important for a party to get immediate help from the court. One spouse may have threatened or inflicted violence, or absconded with all of the community assets. In this situation, a court will set a case down for a quick hearing (usually called a "show cause hearing") to determine the situation of the parties and issue temporary orders that govern the parties until time for the final divorce hearing. In extreme circumstances, a court can issue a temporary restraining order without prior notice to the other spouse. These are normally limited to protective orders, because this procedure does not give the other side an opportunity to be heard before the order is issued.

At a show cause hearing, the wife may also obtain temporary alimony from her husband while the divorce is pending, in order to give her some time to get established on her own. Until 1995, there was no provision for permanent payment of alimony in Texas. In that year, the legislature added a provision for "maintenance" of a spouse with limited earning capacity if the duration of the marriage was 10 years or longer. The duration of support, however, cannot be longer than three years after the order unless the receiving spouse has an incapacitating physical or mental disability.

Division of Property

The court granting a divorce decree must order a division of the community estate between the parties, giving due regard for each person's rights and for their children. It is the judge who decrees a division of the property, even though the trial may have been by jury—the jury's decision in this respect being only advisory. The division does not have to be equal. A court, however, does not have the power to divide the property by divesting one spouse of title to separate real property and awarding it to the other spouse.

Separate and Community Property of the Spouses

Section 3.001 of the Texas Family Code provides that a spouse's separate property consists of:

1. Property owned by the spouse before marriage
2. Property acquired by the spouse during marriage by gift, devise, or descent (inheritance)
3. A recovery for personal injuries sustained by the spouse during marriage, except to the extent the recovery includes damages for loss of earning capacity

Community property consists of the property, other than separate property, acquired by either spouse during marriage. There is a presumption that property possessed during the marriage is community property; the spouse claiming otherwise has the burden of proving that the property is separate.

Most property owned by married couples is community property because most people own very little at the time of their marriage, especially a first marriage. With second and third marriages, this is often not the case. If the couple begins with no property and through their efforts after marriage accumulate property, it is community property—owned equally by the spouses. Community property falls into two classes: special community and general community.

Special community is the part of the community property that one or the other spouse can dispose of, manage, or control, and general community is that part of the community property that is under the joint management and control of both husband and wife. Special community consists of the property a spouse would have owned if single, including personal earnings, revenue from separate property, recoveries from personal injuries, and revenue from all property subject to his or her management, control, and disposition.

Because marriage status in Texas law is considered a partnership, it could be supposed that any property belonging to either spouse could be reached by either spouse's creditors. This marriage partnership, however, may have several property classes:

1. Husband's separate property
2. Wife's separate property
3. General community property
4. Husband's special community property
5. Wife's special community property

For many years, the management of community property was under the sole authority of the husband. Now, the general community property is under the joint management of both spouses, unless they provide otherwise in writing. As already stated, a spouse's special community property is subject to the management of that spouse. The courts have held that neither a spouse's separate property nor special community property is liable for the debts incurred by the other spouse, except for liability in tort and for necessities.

The Practical Application: Separate or Community?

The rules classifying separate and community property seem simple enough. But applying these rules to actual situations can get extremely complex. The courts have evolved additional rules and maxims to help resolve these problems.

For example, what is the status of a home purchased by the husband one year before the marriage, but then paid for by both spouses during 30 years of marriage? "Community property" would appear to be the obvious answer. But under the "inception of title" doctrine, the status of the property is determined as of the date of its acquisition. Here, the home is the husband's separate property. The wife, however, will have a right of reimbursement for her share of the community value put into the home during the marriage.

Suppose at the time of the marriage, the husband has $10,000 in a savings account. It is his separate property. But during the 10 years of marriage, the money is transferred to another savings account and is used by both spouses, with many withdrawals and additions. If, at the time of the divorce, there are $12,000 in the account, does the husband get his $10,000? Probably not. The courts will say that the separate property has been "commingled" with community and has lost its separate character. The entire account is now community property. To win, the husband must be able to "trace" his separate property. Property is presumed to be community unless it can be clearly shown to be separate.

These are only examples. Resolutions of these kinds of problems should be attempted only with the assistance of competent legal counsel.

Change of Name

In a decree for divorce or annulment, the court, for good cause shown, may change the name of either party specifically requesting the change. This is within the court's discretion, however, and a change in name will not be granted if there are children to be affected adversely. A change of name does not release a person from any liability incurred in a previous name or defeat any right which the person held in a previous name.

Children

A divorce does not affect the legitimacy of a couple's children. The court has power in all divorce suits to give the mother or father custody (or managing conservatorship) of the children, having due regard for the parent's prudence and ability and the children's age and sex. The court will be most concerned for the children's welfare. The divorce petition will state whether there are children of the marriage under 18 years of age, and if so, the name, age, and sex of each are shown. The court exercises jurisdiction over these children and their custody, and issues all proper or necessary orders and injunctions.

Until recent years, the issue of custody of a child of tender years was nearly always resolved in favor of the mother. As a general rule, to obtain custody, the father had to prove that the mother was an unfit person. The Texas Family Code, however, now requires the courts to view the qualifications of each parent without regard to the sex of the parent. The issue is to be resolved by what the court or jury considers to be the "best interest of the child."

If the child is 12 years of age or older, he or she may choose his or her managing conservator subject to the approval of the court. In a nonjury trial, the court may interview a younger child in chambers to determine the child's wishes in the matter, but the result of this interview in no way diminishes the discretion or power of the judge to make the decision.

Joint Managing Conservatorship

A court may now appoint parents joint managing conservators of their children if the court finds by a preponderance of the evidence that such an appointment is in the best interest of the children. If the parents agree to this arrangement, the court "shall" appoint them joint managing conservators as long as the agreement meets certain conditions. Such an agreement must designate the conservator who has the sole legal right to determine the residence of the children, and must expressly state the rights and duties of each parent.

The parents have considerable flexibility to reach an agreement that allows maximum contact with their children; the judge, however, retains the right to set aside any agreement that he or she finds not in the best interest of the children. One court, for example, set aside an agreement giving parents alternating weeks with their child, as the parents did not even live in the same school district.

Child Support

The court may order either the father or mother or both to make regular periodical payments, usually monthly or weekly, for the support of their minor children. The amount of child support has long been a major source of contention in divorce cases. In 1987, the Family Code was amended to require the Texas Supreme Court to "adopt guidelines to compute an equitable amount of child support to guide the courts. . . ."

The Supreme Court issued its first "Child Support Guidelines" effective February 4, 1987. These guidelines called for child support to be within a certain range if the obligor's monthly net resources were $4,000 or less. For example, one child meant the payment of from 19%–23% of the obligor's net income.

The legislature subsequently made the guidelines part of the Family Code, and made them quite exact, as follows:

One child: 20% of obligor's net resources
Two children: 25% of obligor's net resources
Three children: 30% of obligor's net resources
Four children: 35% of obligor's net resources
Five through seven children: 40% of obligor's net resources

These guidelines assume that the court will order the obligor to provide health insurance for the children in addition to child support.

A court "shall" follow the guidelines unless there is relevant evidence to justify a variance. In making this determination, a court can consider such things as the needs of the child, the ability of the parents to contribute, available financial resources, and the cost of travel necessary to exercise possession of the child.

Under the guidelines, child support is based on the "net resources" of the parties. Net resources means all income minus social security taxes, federal income tax withholding for a single person claiming one personal exemption, and the standard deduction, union dues, and expenses for health insurance for the obligor's child.

"Income" does not include benefits paid pursuant to aid for families with dependent children or child support from any source. Significantly, the guidelines also give a court the power to determine child support based on the earning potential of the obligor if the court finds that he or she is "intentionally unemployed." Quitting a job to avoid paying child support is not a smart move.

Child support payments, unless changed by subsequent order of the court, will continue until the child reaches the age of 18 or until the end of the school year in which the child graduates from high school, if the child continues to be fully enrolled in an accredited secondary school in a program leading to a high school diploma.

In 1983, a section was added to give relief to persons who owe child support to more than one household. If, at the time of a divorce, a man is already making child support payments to the children of a prior marriage, those children will be taken into account in setting current child support. This is now calculated into the statutory schedule.

Withholding Child Support from Wages

Except for "good cause" or on agreement of the parties, a family court must order that child support be withheld from the obligor's disposable earnings by his or her employer. This will be done in a separate order sent to the employer. If this is not required by the original order, it must go into effect once a delinquency occurs in child support payments.

Standard Orders

The 1989 legislature amended the Family Code to provide guidelines for a "standard" possession order that a court "shall" follow if the child is three years of age or older. Courts retain more flexibility when dealing with younger children.

The law provides that if the possessory conservator resides 100 miles or less from the primary residence of the child, he shall have possession of the child as follows:

1. On weekends from 6 p.m. on the first, third, and fifth Friday of each month until 6 p.m. on the following Sunday, or at the possessory conservator's election from the time the child's school day ends, until 6 p.m. on the following Sunday; and

2. On Wednesdays of each week during the regular school term from 6 p.m. until 8 p.m., or at the possessory conservator's election, from the time the child's school day ends until 8 p.m.

Vacations and holidays are provided for specifically, as follows:

1. The possessory conservator shall have possession of the child in even-numbered years from 6 p.m. on the last school day before the Christmas school vacation begins until noon on December 26th, and the managing conservator shall have possession for the same period in odd-numbered years.

2. The possessory conservator shall have possession of the child in odd-numbered years from noon on December 26th until 6 p.m. on the day before school resumes, and the managing conservator shall have possession for the same period in even-numbered years.

3. The possessory conservator shall have possession of the child in odd-numbered years from 6 p.m. on the Wednesday before Thanksgiving until 6 p.m. on the following Sunday, and the managing conservator shall have possession for the same period in even-numbered years.

4. The possessory conservator shall have possession of the child in even-numbered years from 6 p.m. on the last school day before the school's spring vacation begins until 6 p.m. on

the day before school resumes, and the managing conservator shall have possession for the same period in odd-numbered years.

The statute continues with detailed guidelines for summer visitation, giving the possessory conservator thirty days, with provisions for visitation during this time by the managing conservator. It also sets out exact visitation times when the possessory conservator lives more than 100 miles from the child's residence.

While these provisions are typical of many existing divorce decrees, never before have such details been defined by statute. Apparently the legislature was trying to reduce the volume of contested cases by making support and visitation less subject to a court's discretion.

Typical Post-Decree Difficulties

Problems involving children do not end with the divorce decree. What if the parent having custody of the child moves out of the state? The other then feels cheated because he is still being required to pay child support yet is no longer able to exercise regular visitation.

The order of the court for support may require that the parent having custody not remove the children from the county or state without permission of the court. Generally, such permission will be granted when there is a valid reason for the move, such as a job transfer. Both parents should be careful in this regard, because it is now a felony of the third degree to remove a child from the state and retain him for more than seven days in violation of a court order disposing of the child's custody.

Another problem arises when the parent ordered to make support payments leaves the state, generally the father, and the mother finds that the cost of pursuing him exceeds the benefits to be gained for the children. Of course, the parent who leaves the state has a right to do so, but it is nevertheless contempt of court to fail to make the ordered support payments. The mother who has custody of the children and is entitled to receive the support payments may follow him into the state of his new residence and bring suit against him there to enforce the order of the Texas court; or she may have him placed under orders of the court in the place of his residence by means of the Uniform Reciprocal Enforcement of Support Act, which is now in effect in most states. A person in default of child support payments is subject to being jailed for his failure—not for the debt he owes, but because he is in violation of a court order.

Continuing Disputes: Enforcement and Modification

The Texas Family Code provides that once a court acquires jurisdiction of a suit affecting the parent-child relationship, that court retains continuing, exclusive jurisdiction of the case unless the parties establish a new principal residence outside of Texas. This means that in most cases, after the divorce is final, continuing disputes go back to the original court.

Enforcement: Contempt of Court

A court has numerous remedies available for enforcement of its judgments and decrees. In family law cases, the most frequently used vehicle is an action for contempt of court. The Family Code states that, after notice and hearing, any decree of the court for child support may be enforced by contempt. A person found guilty of contempt may be fined up to $500 or confined in jail for up to six months, or both.

Because of the quasi-criminal nature of contempt proceedings, the pleadings must be specific and exact. Each act of contempt must be alleged. Courts today, however, seem more willing than in the past to jail a person who has failed to pay child support as ordered.

Modification of Conservatorship and Support

As a general rule, a party is not allowed to modify the substance of a judgment or decree of a court of law. There is a need for finality of judgments. Otherwise, disputes would never come to an end. Family law is a major exception to this rule. Chapter 156 of the Family Code sets out the provisions and conditions for modification.

The party seeking modification must first prove that since the date of the decree the circumstances of the parties or children have "materially and substantially changed." The party can't get a decree changed just because he doesn't like it. It varies from case to case. An increase in salary, increased expenses for children, or loss of a job are factors that often lead to a modification of child support.

It is usually more difficult to establish substantial change when modification of conservatorship is sought. Added to this is the additional burden of proving that a continuation of the existing situation ". . . would be injurious to the welfare of the child . . ." and the appointment of a new managing conservator would be a "positive improvement." This burden of proof is difficult to meet. A motion to modify child support is more likely to succeed since passage of the statutory child support guidelines, which are presumed to be reasonable and in the best interest of the child.

It is, of course, much easier to modify a decree if the parties are in agreement. An agreed order modifying a decree will normally be approved by the court, unless the judge believes it is not in the best interest of the child. Once signed and entered, an agreed order is just as binding and enforceable as any other judgment.

Actions for Paternity

For many years in Texas, the biological father of a child born out of wedlock had no legal rights as to that child. The child could be put up for adoption without any notice to him. Conversely, the mother had great difficulty in getting child support from the father. This is now changed because of decisions by the United States Supreme Court and amendments to the Texas Family Code.

In two significant cases in 1972, the Supreme Court ruled that biological fathers have a constitutional right to notice of legal action affecting their children. The Court also ruled that a state could not deny to illegitimate children rights accorded to other children just because the child's father was not married to its mother. As a result, most states have procedures for a man to sue to be recognized judicially as the father of his child. The mother can also sue to establish, legally, the paternity of the biological father. Once established, the usual rights and duties flow from the parent-child relationship (child support, visitation, etc.).

The key to a modern paternity action is the method of establishing paternity. In 1983, the Family Code was amended to allow for the results of certain blood-testing procedures to be used in court, and gave courts authority to require parties to submit to such testing. This was expanded in 1989 to include testing procedures in addition to those based on blood. This was made possible by scientific advances that are able to show statistical probabilities of paternity approaching certainty—not only the negative proof that an individual is *not* the father, but also the positive proof that a particular individual *is* the father. The courts are even allowing these tests as evidence to rebut paternity when conception occurred during marriage. This would have been unheard of several years ago.

Sale of the Homestead

If the homestead is the separate property of one of the spouses, or is community property, both spouses must join together to transfer the title or mortgage it, if they are living together and both remain capable of transacting business.

If the homestead is the *separate* property of one of the spouses and the other spouse has been judicially declared incompetent, then the homestead may be sold, conveyed, or encumbered without the incompetent spouse's consent. If the homestead is the separate property of a spouse and (a) the other spouse is incompetent, whether decreed so or not; (b) the other spouse disappears and his or her whereabouts remain unknown to the owner; (c) the other spouse permanently abandons the homestead; or (d) the spouses are permanently separated, then after the expiration of 60 days, the owner may file a sworn petition in the district court describing the homestead and the facts that make it desirable to sell or mortgage the property. After required notices are given and a hearing has taken place, the court may authorize the owner to sell or mortgage the homestead without the other spouse's consent.

If the homestead is the spouses' *community* property and one spouse has been decreed incompetent by a court having jurisdiction, then the competent spouse may sell or mortgage the homestead without the other spouse's consent.

If the homestead is the *community* property of the spouses and (a) one of the spouses is incompetent, whether or not decreed so; (b) a spouse disappears and his or her whereabouts remain unknown to the other spouse; (c) one spouse permanently abandons the homestead and the other spouse; or (d) one spouse permanently abandons the homestead and the spouses are permanently separated, then after 60 days, the competent spouse, the remaining spouse, the abandoned spouse, or the spouse who has not abandoned the homestead in case of a permanent separation may file a sworn petition in the district court describing the property and stating the facts that make it desirable for the spouse filing the petition to sell, transfer, or mortgage the homestead without the joinder of the other spouse.

After the required notices and a hearing, the court may issue an order permitting the petitioning spouse to sell, transfer, or mortgage the homestead. The court can enter other orders and place restraints it considers desirable or equitable upon the petitioning spouse, because it is also the duty of the court to protect the interest of the absent spouse.

The Homestead

The Texas Homestead Act is based upon the political philosophy that once a person has acquired a home, he or she and his or her family should not be deprived of it by forced sale, regardless of how indiscreet, foolish, or reckless he or she may have been in managing his financial affairs. Previous generations became sensitive to their fellow men who suffered from starvation and despair after they were driven from their homes by creditors. They must have viewed the homestead law as the next logical step after the constitutional provision that no person should be imprisoned for debt.

The Texas legislature adopted measures to protect a person against himself. Until recently a person could not mortgage his or her homestead except for repairs, improvements, or additions to it. Banks and mortgage companies would not lend money on a homestead except for improvements because loans for any other purpose would not be enforced. In 1995, however, the people of Texas approved a constitutional amendment that allows individuals to seek additional types of loans secured by the homestead.

Our Texas Homestead Act was inspired by exemptions from forced sale contained in Spanish and Mexican laws, but the law itself is a Texas creation. The first homestead exemption was enacted by the Third Congress of the Republic of Texas on January 26, 1839.

Article XVI, Section 50, of the Texas Constitution provides that a family's homestead, or that of an unmarried adult male or female, shall be protected from forced sale for the payment of all debts except the money used to purchase the homestead, or a part of the purchase money, the taxes due on the homestead, or for work and materials used in constructing improvements. In the latter case, the lien will be valid only when the work and materials are contracted for in writing, with the spouse's consent given in the same way it is required in making a sale and conveyance of the homestead. It also provides that the owner, if a married person, shall not sell the homestead without the spouse's consent. He or she must join in the sale to make it valid.

In 1995, Section 50 was amended to allow the extension of credit to be secured by a voluntary lien on the homestead created under a written agreement with the consent of the owner and the owner's spouse, provided the loan cannot bring the total indebtedness against the home to more than 80 percent of the face market value of the homestead. Such a lien can be foreclosed only by court order. Lenders must comply with a number of fairly technical requirements in order to obtain a valid lien. Of course, the taxes against the homestead create a lien against it, but this does not represent a voluntary mortgage given by the owners.

What Constitutes the Homestead

The homestead of a family in the country may consist of as much as 200 acres with improvements, and the land may be in one or more parcels. A single, adult person may claim only 100 acres as a rural homestead. If a man and his family live on a 1,000-acre tract and call it their home, they would have an exemption only for 200 acres, including the house.

The homestead for a family or single person in a city, town, or village shall consist of not more than one acre of land, which may be in one or more lots, together with all residences and other improvements on the land.

So, once the homestead has been established, either in the city or in the country, there are only three kinds of liens that can be foreclosed against it: (a) the lien given to secure the payment of the purchase money, or part of it; (b) the lien given to secure payment for improvements (such as additions to the residence and its appurtenances, repairs, painting, etc.), which must be signed by both spouses, and the writing must have been executed before the work is commenced; and (c) the tax lien for taxes against the homestead. The proceeds from the sale of a homestead are not subject to seizure for a creditor's claim for six months after the date of sale. To receive the full protection of this statute, a person should file a homestead designation with the county clerk.

The following are also exempt from forced sales:

1. One or more lots for a place of burial of the dead.
2. Personal property not to exceed an aggregate fair market value of not more than $30,000 for a single adult not a member of a family, or $60,000 for a family, if included among the following:
   (a) Furnishings of a home, including family heirlooms and provisions for consumption;
   (b) Farming and ranching vehicles and implements, tools, equipment, books, and apparatus, including boats and other vehicles used in a trade or profession; wearing apparel, two firearms, athletic and sporting equipment, including bicycles, and jewelry not to exceed in value 25 percent of the above aggregate limitations;
   (c) A two-wheeled, three-wheeled, or four-wheeled motor vehicle for each member of a family or single adult who holds a driver's license or who relies on another person to operate the vehicle;
   (d) The following animals and forage on hand for their consumption: two horses, mules, or donkeys and a saddle, blanket, and bridle for each; 12 head of cattle; 60 head of other types of livestock; and 120 fowl;
   (e) Household pets;

(f) The present value of any life insurance policy to the extent that a member or members of the family of the insured or a dependent of a single insured adult claiming the exemption is a beneficiary of the policy; or

(g) Current wages for personal services (except for child support) and professionally prescribed health aids are exempt, regardless of value.

Even though this statute was recently amended, it still has a rural emphasis.

Obviously, there is room for interpretation by the courts over whether specific items are included in the various categories. There is apparently now no limit on the number of automobiles and light trucks that can be exempted, as long as the monetary limits are not exceeded.

There is another important aspect of this law: Federal courts can follow the Texas statutes in bankruptcy proceedings in this state, and allow the same exemptions and substitutions that the state courts do in estate and foreclosure proceedings.

In 1987, the Texas legislature added an additional exemption to protect from levy a person's interest in stock bonuses, pensions, profit-sharing, annuities, or similar plans and contracts, including retirement plans. To qualify for the exemption, the plan must be in compliance with the applicable provisions of the Internal Revenue Code of 1986.

Guardians and Adoption

Often guardians must be appointed to take care of other persons or to manage their estates, as in the case of:

1. Minors;
2. An adult individual who, because of a physical or mental condition, is substantially unable to provide food, clothing,

or shelter for himself or herself, to care for the individual's own physical health, or to manage the individual's own financial affairs;

3. A missing person; or
4. A person who must have a guardian appointed to receive funds from any governmental source.

In all such situations, the law provides for appointment of a guardian by the county judge, who is also the probate judge, in the county where the person or persons may reside, and a guardian may be appointed for the person or for the estate of any such person. The judge may require whatever bond of the guardian that he considers necessary to protect the estate. In small counties, the county judge may transfer contested cases over to the jurisdiction of the district court.

In the state's more populous counties, there is a probate judge in addition to the county judge. The county judge is concerned with the county's fiscal or business matters, while the probate judge is concerned with such matters as guardianships, probate, and administration of estates.

Persons Disqualified to Serve as Guardians

The following persons shall not be appointed guardians: minors; persons whose conduct is notoriously bad; incompetents; or those who are parties to, or whose father or mother is a party to, a lawsuit that determines the welfare of the person for whom or for whose estate a guardian is to be appointed.

Also excluded from guardianship are those who are indebted to the person for whom or for whose estate a guardian is to be appointed, unless they pay the debt prior to the appointment; or who are asserting any claim to any property, real or personal, adverse to the person for whom or for whose estate the appointment is sought; and those who, because of inexperience, lack of education, or other good reason, are shown to be incapable of properly and prudently managing and controlling the ward or his estate.

Adoption

Often, it is desirable that minor children be adopted by persons who are able and willing to care for them. Some of the circumstances, but not all, that present a need for adoption of children are: (a) the death of both parents; (b) both parents desert their children; (c) the parents are incapable of taking care of the children; or (d) a child is born out of wedlock to a mother who is unable to care for it or perhaps does not desire to keep it and care for it. In this last instance, quite often the father cannot be found, or he may be a minor, or for other reasons cannot be made to take parental responsibility for the child. It is a fact, too, that there are more families seeking children to adopt than there are children to place with them.

In 1973, a new adoption statute was enacted by the Texas legislature as part of the Texas Family Code. It simplifies and clarifies prior law, and gives the adoptive parents much greater security. The statutory procedures are quite specific and must be complied with. Attempts to avoid these requirements can lead to bitter disappointment for prospective adoptive parents. In addition, the legislature added a provision to the penal code making it a crime for one to offer to accept, agree to accept, or accept anything of value for the delivery of possession of a child for the purposes of adoption; or to offer to give, agree to give, or give anything of value for acquiring a child for the purpose of adoption. There are three exceptions: (a) fees paid to licensed child placement agencies, (b) fees paid to attorneys or physicians for usual services, and (c) reimbursement of legal or medical expenses incurred for the benefit of the child.

Before a child can be adopted, all existing parental rights must be terminated. In some instances, this means the bringing of two lawsuits: the first to terminate parental rights and the second for the adoption of the child—though in most cases the two causes of action can be combined in one lawsuit.

The father of an illegitimate child may be included in the definition of "parent" in the Family Code as a presumed biological father; therefore one is required to prove against him the statutory grounds justifying a termination. He is entitled to notice of any lawsuit affecting the status of the child.

Termination of the parent-child relationship will be granted by the court if there is a finding that termination is in the best interest of the child, and if the parent has:

1. Voluntarily left the child alone or in the possession of another (not the parent) and expressed an intent not to return.
2. Voluntarily left the child alone or in possession of another (not the parent) without providing for adequate support of the child, and remained away at least three months.
3. Voluntarily left the child alone or in possession of another (even a parent) without providing adequate support of the child and remained away for a period of at least six months.
4. Knowingly placed or allowed the child to remain in conditions or surroundings that endangered the physical or emotional well-being of the child.
5. Engaged in conduct or knowingly placed the child with persons who engaged in conduct that endangered the physical or emotional well-being of the child.
6. Failed to support the child in accordance with his ability during a period of one year ending within six months of the date of the filing of the petition.
7. Abandoned the child without identifying the child or furnishing means of identification, and the child's identity cannot be ascertained by the exercise of reasonable diligence.
8. Voluntarily abandoned the mother of the child beginning at a time during her pregnancy and continuing through the

birth and failed to provide adequate support or medical care during the period of abandonment before the birth of the child, and remained apart from the child or failed to support the child since the birth.

9. Refused to submit to a reasonable court order regarding an investigation of child welfare into the circumstances of a child.

10. Has been the major cause of the failure of the child to be enrolled in school or the child's absence from home without consent of his parent or guardian for a substantial length of time.

11. Has executed an irrevocable affidavit of relinquishment of parental rights.

12. Has been adjudicated criminally responsible for the death or serious injury of another of his/her children.

13. Has had his/her parental-child relationship terminated as to another child because his/her conduct violated number 4 or 5 above.

14. Constructively abandoned a child who has been under the authority and control of the Department of Protective and Regulatory Services for at least six months.

15. Failed to obey a court order that established actions necessary for the parent to obtain the return of the child.

16. Used a controlled substance in a manner that endangered the health or safety of the child.

17. Knowingly engaged in criminal conduct resulting in the parent's imprisonment for at least two years.

18. Been the cause of the child being born addicted to alcohol or a controlled substance (other than one obtained by prescription).

These grounds seem straightforward enough, yet contested adoptions are difficult to win. This is because courts have taken a strict approach to the "best interest" standard. Even if the petitioner establishes one of the categories such as non-support, he or she must still prove that it is in the best interest of the minor to terminate the parental relationship. Courts have pointed out that, unlike conservatorship, termination is final and irrevocable. It forever divests the parent and child of all legal rights with respect to each other except for the child's right to inherit. In 1980, the Texas Supreme Court ruled that the proper standard of proof in a termination case is "clear and convincing evidence"—a more difficult burden than the usual "preponderance of the evidence" standard.

An adoption proceeding is started by filing a petition by an adult person or persons in a district court (a) in the county where the petitioners reside; (b) in the county where the child or children to be adopted reside; or (c) if the child or children are placed with a child-placing institution, in the county where that institution is located.

After the petition has been filed, the court clerk will mail a certified copy to the executive director of the State Department of Public Welfare. The executive director or the court will then require a report for the court's information showing all of the pertinent facts about the petitioners and the child or children to be adopted. Of course, the court must be satisfied that the child or children are so unfortunately situated that the proposed adoption is desirable and that the petitioners are suitable persons for the adoption.

The court may award the temporary care and custody of a child to the petitioner, but an adoption is not permitted under the law until after the child has lived in the petitioner's home for six months. The reason for such a rule is obvious. Before the child is awarded to the petitioner, the court will set a hearing for the case, and the petitioner will be questioned in the presence of the judge at the hearing. The hearing must not be held less than 40 days or more than 60 days after the clerk mails a copy of the petition to the executive director of the State Department of Public Welfare. If the child to be adopted is 14 years of age or older, then the child's written consent to the adoption and his presence at the hearing are required.

Status of Adopted Child

When a minor child is adopted, it becomes the child of the adoptive parents just as if it had been born to them. The adoptive parents owe it the same duties that they owe to their natural child, and they are obligated by law to furnish the adopted child food, clothing, a home, schooling, and such other attentions as they are required by law to give to their natural child. The adoptive parents are entitled to the child's services and the money that it may earn while a minor, and they are entitled to its company and to have control over it.

The natural parent who gives the child up for adoption by others loses the right to inherit from the child, but the adopted child does not by its adoption lose the right to inherit from its natural parents. Obviously, parents who have had their parental rights terminated no longer have a right of access or visitation with their child. Yet, the Family Code provides that the natural grandparents of the child may continue to have visitation rights with the child.

2. Wills and Estates of Decedents

Under Texas law, if a person owning property dies without making a valid will, all of that person's estate vests immediately in his or her heirs. It does not go to the state. Establishing this to the satisfaction of third parties can be a problem if there is no will. To properly handle the estate, someone must file for a formal administration. This procedure is costly to the estate, resulting in necessary and extensive proceedings and expenses that consume a high percentage of the estate's assets, and it does not compare favorably with the independent administration under a properly executed will.

In such a situation, the court will appoint an administrator, who must give bond, with the bond's cost being chargeable against the estate. The administrator is allowed a fee for his services and the fee, or fees, are payable out of the estate. The administrator must have legal assistance, and the attorney's fees are also payable out of the estate.

If any property of the estate is to be sold, or if money is to be borrowed to defray expenses, or almost any other transaction is to be made, a petition must be filed with the court and notices must be given. Next, there must be a hearing on the petition where proof must be given to the court that the proposed action in the petition is necessary or beneficial to the estate.

If the court is convinced, an order will be issued authorizing the administrator to do what he has requested of the court. A report must then be made to the court showing what was done after its order, and then the court issues an order approving what has been done.

Wills

Under Texas law, a person who is capable of making a will may dispose of his estate by a duly executed will, which becomes effective upon its probate after that person's death. A will is a declaration by a person, usually in writing, directing how he would have his estate disposed of after his death. Wills fall into three classifications:

1. A will written entirely in the handwriting of the person making it. It does not require any signing by witnesses. This is known as a holographic will.
2. A will that is typed or printed, usually prepared by an attorney, for execution by the one making the will. This kind requires two witnesses, but there may be more, who will sign in the presence of the testator (the one making the will) and in the presence of each other. It is now possible to attach a self-proving affidavit, which is executed before a notary public. When this is done properly the witnesses do not have to appear and testify when the will is probated.
3. A will that is made without a writing as in the situation where a person is near death and calls witnesses to hear him state how he wishes his estate disposed of after his death. If the estate of the testator in this case exceeds $30, then there must be three witnesses who hear the testator speak the words that compose the will. To qualify as a witness to a will, one must be of sound mind and over 14 years of age.

Who May Make a Will

Article 57 of the Texas Probate Code provides that every person who has attained the age of 18 years, is or has been lawfully married, or is a member of the armed forces of the United States or the auxiliaries thereof at the time the will is made, being of sound mind, shall have the power to make a last will and testament.

Advantages of a Will

A will can serve many good purposes. One who owns any property should make his will at an early date, always aware that he can revoke or change the will at any subsequent time when he is still of sound mind. He can make a new one, or add to the old one by codicil if he prefers. By making a will, a person can choose the individual or individuals who are to manage his affairs after his death, can give his property to the persons or institutions of his own choosing, can extend or shorten the time that may otherwise be used in completing the business of the estate, and can control to a considerable degree the expense of carrying out the will's terms.

As mentioned previously, one type of will is that written wholly in the testator's handwriting. One should remember, however, that it does no good to make a will if it cannot be admitted to probate, or if it does not accomplish the testator's purposes. That is why competent legal advice is important. This is especially true as one's estate grows larger and more complex.

The Independent Administration

Almost all wills prepared by Texas lawyers provide for independent administrations. Such wills not only dispose of the testator's estate and all of his property, but also appoint an independent executor or independent executrix, without bond. These wills provide that, after the will is admitted to probate, and an inventory and appraisement and a list of claims have been filed, the cause of action can be dropped from the court docket. This limits the court's functions by removing the estate from the court's supervision and placing the estate in the hands of the person, bank, or trust company named in the will to take charge of the estate and carry out the will's terms.

Of course, the will must be probated, and that means that it must be proven to the probate judge's satisfaction that the will is the last, true, and valid will of the person making it. Roughly, the preliminary procedure to place a will in probate is:

1. The executor named in the will obtains possession of it and places it with an attorney for probate.
2. The attorney draws up a petition to the court stating that the testator is dead and that the court has jurisdiction of the cause, alleging the necessary facts: the testator left a valid will, which is attached to the petition; and in the will the testator appointed an independent executor without bond, etc. The attorney then requests that the will be admitted to probate.
3. The court clerk issues the necessary notices and gives them to the county sheriff or a constable for posting.
4. The officer posts the notices as required by law and reports to the court indicating how he has published the notices.
5. After the necessary time lapse, which is at least 10 full days after the posting date, the attorney goes into court and generally the independent executor appointed in the will accompanies him, and the attorney offers the necessary proof to the court to show that it is a valid last will and that he is offering for probate.

The proof that the court will require is: that the one who made the will (the testator) is dead and that four years have not elapsed since his death and prior to the date of filing the application; that the court has jurisdiction and venue over the estate; that citation has been served and returned in the manner and for the length of time required by the probate code; that the person who made the will was at the time he made it qualified to do so; that the testator executed the will with the formalities and solemnities and under the circumstances required by law to make it a valid will; that the will has not been revoked by the testator; and that the person making the application is the person named in the will as independent executor (or independent executrix) and that that person is not disqualified to receive letters testamentary.

If all of this proof is made at the hearing to the court's satisfaction, the court will enter an order prepared by the attorney and presented to the court for signature admitting the will to probate. Letters testamentary will be issued to the person appointed in the will as soon as that person has signed the oath required by law, and the court, in the same order, will appoint one or more appraisers to evaluate the estate and make a list of claims. In small estates with little or no real property, the court will often waive the appointment of appraisers.

As a matter of practice, the independent executor, with the attorney's help, will inventory the estate, and will make a list of claims or debts against the estate and a list of claims in favor of the estate. Both the executor and the attorney will sign the inventory and lists and give them, along with any changes they think should be made, to appraisers for consideration and for their signatures. When this appraisement and list of claims have been duly signed and filed with the court clerk, the attorney will ascertain from it, based upon the estate's value, whether there are taxes on the estate that must be paid to the State of Texas and to the federal government. The attorney will prepare and file the necessary reports, showing the taxes due, if any, and the reports must be signed by the person appointed in the will as independent executor (or executrix).

After these procedures are completed, the court will drop the case from the court docket. The independent executor (or executrix), after signing the oath, is entitled to take over the estate to manage and control it. Of course, the estate is still charged with the debts that may have been created against it, and creditors have a year in which to file their claims with the executor so that they will be properly classed and put in line for payment out of the estate's funds. A creditor who fails to file his claim within that time will have consideration only if assets are left over after discharging those claims that were filed on time.

The will may be written so that it is clear that the independent executor's function is to complete the affairs of the estate and deliver the estate to those who are shown in the will to be entitled to it. Quite often a man will make his will and appoint his wife as independent executrix, giving all of his property to her. Conversely, a wife frequently will make her will and appoint her husband as independent executor and give all of her property to him. In these cases, the one appointed and receiving the property will attempt to complete the proceedings as soon as possible and then own the property in his or her own name.

On the other hand, a person's business and his estate may prevent such quick action. He may choose to place his estate with a trustee or trustees with authority to manage and control it. The trustee can invest and reinvest the estate's funds so that an income is made over a period of time. The trustee can be instructed to pay or deliver the income to persons named in the will, with further provisions that, at the end of a certain time or upon the occurrence of a specified event, the assets of the estate are to be distributed to persons named in the will.

Moreover, a person having a considerable estate may have the purpose of saving taxes or postponing taxes upon his estate or a portion of it, and through careful planning with the aid of his attorney and his tax adviser much can be accomplished. In some instances, it is advantageous to set up trusts and put them in effect while the person making them is still living. He can manage these trusts during his lifetime, and in his will he can appoint a trustee to carry on after his death. This arrangement can sometimes save substantial taxes or result in the postponement of taxes.

Probate of Will as Muniment of Title

In some situations, the estate is so well-ordered that there is no need for an administration. If the estate owes no debts other than those secured by real estate, the will can be probated for Muniment of Title only. When this is done, no executor or administrator is appointed by the court and no letters are issued. A certified copy of the will and the order of probate is sufficient legal authority for those holding property of the decedent to turn it over to the persons named as beneficiaries in the will. This procedure is simpler and less expensive than a normal probate.

The Unwritten or Nuncupative Will

The unwritten or nuncupative will provided for under the law is the least used and the most unsatisfactory will form. It can be established only when pronounced during a person's last illness, he or she dies at home, the value of the estate is minimal, and it is witnessed by at least three credible witnesses. This form of will is rarely used.

The court will be cautious, and properly so, in admitting an unwritten will to probate because there is always room for doubt and uncertainty. In addition to the usual requirements of proof for a will, the law requires that a nuncupative will cannot be proved before 14 days after the death of the testator, or until interested parties have been notified and have had opportunities to contest the will. In addition, the will cannot be proved after six months from the date the alleged testamentary words were spoken.

What to do with a Will after it is Made

A will, after it is executed, should be kept in a safe place where the person named as executor or executrix can find it so that it can be presented for probate, because a will must be probated to be effective. A safe deposit box in a bank is a common place for keeping wills. A person named in a will as executor or executrix can, after the testator's death upon proper application to the probate court, obtain an order to the bank where the will is kept to open the box and make an inventory of the box's contents. If the will is found, the bank must deliver it to the court or to the person named in the order so that it may be submitted for probate. After the will has been admitted to probate and the executor has qualified, the executor can present the bank his letters testamentary issued by the court clerk and take charge of the box's contents.

It is now permissible for a bank, or other holder of a will for safekeeping, to deliver the will to the executor named in the will without a court order, but it must get a receipt and keep a copy of the document.

Self-Proved Wills

If one making a will uses witnesses considerably older than himself, those he could reasonably expect to outlive, it may later be found that his witnesses are no longer available to prove this will. On the other hand, if he uses young people as witnesses, they may move away, possibly to a foreign country, and it would be costly or impossible to get them to return to give testimony at the time of the testator's death.

While there is a method of proving a will by taking the witness' deposition, this is costly and time-consuming. For these and other reasons, the law was changed to provide for the "self-proved" will. This is done by having the testator and witnesses execute an affidavit before a notary public at the time the will is executed. The language in the self-proving affidavit must meet specific statutory requirements, therefore legal assistance from an attorney is needed. Today, virtually all wills prepared by attorneys are drawn in this manner.

While the self-proven will carries its own proof of execution, it, as any other will, must be probated to become effective after the death of the testator, and it is necessary to present to the court proof of the death of the testator and the date and place of death to establish the jurisdiction and venue of the court in which the will is offered for probate.

Change by Codicil

It is inherent that wills can be changed at any time while the testator is living and still of sound mind. A person making a will today can make another one tomorrow, next week, next month, next year, or years later, but it is the last one that is effective upon the testator's death. A person may be satisfied with the will he has made, except for one or more things he has decided that he would like to include in it or things he forgot to put in it when the will was executed. The change may be made by destroying the old will and making a new one, or it may be made by a codicil, which is an addition.

Because the codicil will become a part of the will, it must be made under the same rules that govern the making of wills. When it is made and attached to the will, it becomes effective with the probate of the will after the testator's death, the same as if it had originally been written into the body of the will. A self-proving affidavit can be attached to the codicil just as to the original will.

Change in Will Caused by Divorce

If a person makes a will and later is divorced, the provisions of the will concerning the divorced spouse are ineffective. For example, a man and his wife each makes a will, and each makes the other a beneficiary or legatee of a portion of his estate. The husband appoints the wife as his independent executrix and the wife appoints the husband as her independent executor, and each appoints the other as guardian of his or her minor children. After such a will is made, if a divorce is granted, these provisions of the will are not effective.

Right of Survivorship in Joint Accounts

A frequent problem arises when a person who dies has a joint bank account with another person who is not a beneficiary under the deceased's will. Does the joint nature of the account constitute a gift of that account to the other person? Not unless there is more than just the joint account. For survivorship to occur, there must be a written agreement that states substantially as follows: "On the death of one party to a joint account, all sums in the account on the date of death vest in and belong to the surviving party as his or her separate property and estate." Of course, the other party can always show the extent to which he or she owned funds in the joint account before the death of the decedent.

Passage of Estate of Testator to Descendants of his Legatees

If one making a valid will devises or bequeaths to his or her child or children or other descendants an estate or any kind of interest in an estate, and the devisees should die before the testator and leave children or descendants who do survive the testator, the devise or legacy will go to the children in the same manner as if the devisees had survived the testator and died intestate. This rule does not apply to those who are not children or other descendants of the testator. The child or other descendant of the original heir who is not a child or descendant of the testator will not receive the devise or legacy. For example: If the testator named as one of his devisees a person who is not related to him and that unrelated devisee dies before the testator, the children of the unrelated devisee will not be entitled to the legacy.

The Right of Election

Sometimes a person making a will wants to dispose of property that is not his own. It most often happens in the case of community property, and it generally is the husband who makes such a will. He may honestly feel that he knows best how to provide for his wife, or he may not know that he cannot dispose of his wife's part of the community property without her consent, or he may not understand the law governing community property.

Suppose a man and his wife have considerable community property consisting of land with a home on it, livestock, cash in bank, stocks and bonds, etc., all of which is community property, and the man dies. His will provides that the wife shall have the use of the home and its furnishings, as long as she does not remarry, together with a monthly sum of money to be paid to her from the money in the bank as long as she remains single, and then he gives to each child part of the land which is valuable and divides up the stocks and bonds among his children and two or three of his sisters.

Now the wife owns one-half of all the two possessed at the time of his death, and she has certain other rights as the survivor in community, such as the right to live in and use the home as long as she lives—his half of it, as well as her half of it. She might consult her attorney as to her rights and decide that she will elect to repudiate the will and claim her community rights. Thereby, she will keep the home for her own use and will have certain benefits out of the community assets and a fee-simple ownership of one-half of all of the other property. By this election, she will defeat a large part of the will, but she has a perfect right to do so.

It is not the wife alone, however, who has the right of election. In any case where one making a will seeks to dispose of property not his or her own while at the same time making that other person, whose property is to be disposed of, a beneficiary under the will, then an election is available to that person.

This principle of the law is easy to understand by a simple illustration. Al says to Bill, "I am going to give you my black horse, and I am going to take your Shetland pony and give it to Carl." Now, obviously Al cannot dispose of Bill's pony without his consent, but Bill cannot accept the black horse and keep the pony. If he is going to receive the gift he must comply with the condition imposed with it. Bill has the right of election. He can accept the black horse and give up the pony, or he can keep the pony and refuse the black horse.

Or suppose that John Doe, who is a widower with three children, marries Mary Roe and they have one child, John Doe, Jr. Neither the husband nor the wife has any appreciable property before their marriage, but through the years they amass a considerable community estate. Mary dies intestate and later John dies leaving a will in which he treats all of the property as if it belonged to him and he provides that it shall be divided equally among his four children.

Now, John Doe, Jr., being the only lawful heir of his deceased mother, Mary, who owned one-half of all of the community property, has the right of election. He may elect to receive under the will and give up his right of inheritance from his mother. But if he is well advised, he will repudiate the will and claim by inheritance from his mother, which he has a right to do.

Descent and Distribution

In Texas, a person may dispose of his property as he chooses. Of course, while he is living, he can sell it or give it to whomever he chooses. By making a will he can choose those who will have his property after his death, but if he fails to make a valid will, the law directs the handling of his estate upon his death. If a man dies without leaving a valid will he dies "intestate," and the laws of descent and distribution deal with this kind of estate. It is not enough that the husband tells the wife, or the wife tells the husband, "In event of my death, all of my estate is to belong to you," or "This part of my estate is to be yours and that part of my estate is to belong to the children."

Such a statement does not transfer the title nor give the person to whom it is made any right of claim to the estate after the death of the one making the statement. It does not benefit any who are mentioned as intended beneficiaries. If a person intends to make a will but fails to do so, his expressed intention, however often it may have been repeated, is powerless after his death.

We shall now consider the provisions of the law with respect to estates of decedents who do not make wills or that part of a person's estate not disposed of by will, because sometimes a person makes a will and fails to dispose of all of his estate. In this case, that part of his estate not disposed of by the will is ruled according to the laws of descent and distribution.

Persons Who Inherit from an Intestate

1. *If the Intestate Leaves No Husband or Wife.* Where a person owning property dies intestate, leaving no husband or wife, his property passes and is inherited by his kindred in the following course: (a) to his children and their descendants (Figure 2.1); (b) if he has no children and there are no descendants of his children, then to his father and mother (Figure 2.2), in equal portions; but if only the father or mother survives the intestate (Figures 2.3 and 2.4), then one-half of the estate passes to that parent who is living, and the other one-half passes to the brothers and sisters of the deceased (the intestate), and to their descendants; but if there are no brothers nor sisters nor their descendants, then the whole estate is inherited by the surviving father or mother; (c) if there is neither a father nor a mother surviving, and there are brothers and sisters (Figure 2.5), and their descendants, then the whole estate passes to these brothers and sisters and their

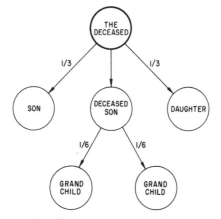

Figure 2.1. The distribution of separate property when the deceased is not survived by a husband or wife and dies intestate (leaves no will). The property will first go to the deceased's children and their descendants.

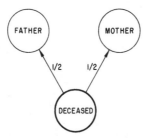

Figure 2.2. If there are no children or descendants, the deceased's parents inherit equal shares of the separate property.

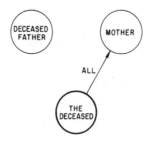

Figure 2.3. If only one parent survives and the deceased parent is not survived by any descendants, the whole goes to the surviving parent.

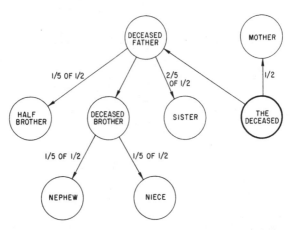

Figure 2.4. If only one parent survives but the deceased parent has living heirs, then half of the estate goes to the surviving parent and the other half goes to the heirs of the deceased parent.

descendants (if a brother or sister is deceased leaving surviving children, the part that would have passed to that brother or sister is inherited by that one's children); (d) if the deceased has none of the kindred mentioned above (Figures 2.6, 2.7, and 2.8), then his estate is divided into two equal portions, one of which passes to the paternal kindred (those on the father's side) and the other to the maternal kindred (those on the mother's side) in the following course:

(text continued on page 52)

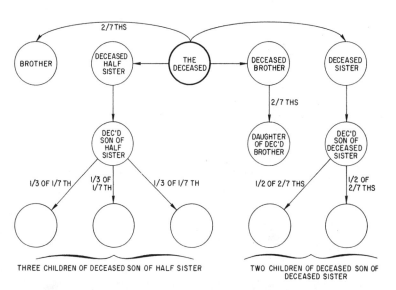

Figure 2.5. If the deceased has no descendants and neither the father nor the mother survives, the whole of the estate will pass to the brothers and sisters of the deceased and their descendants.

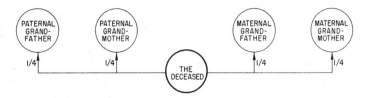

Figure 2.6. If the deceased has none of the previously mentioned relatives but is survived by grandparents, the estate will be divided into two equal portions, one of which shall go to the maternal grandparents and the other to the paternal grandparents.

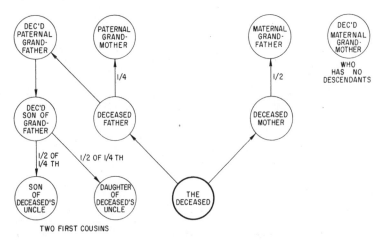

Figure 2.7. If the deceased has no descendants and is not survived by father or mother or their descendants but is survived by grandparents and their descendants on each side, then as before, the estate will be divided into two equal portions, one of which will go to the maternal grandparents and their descendants and the other to the paternal grandparents and their descendants.

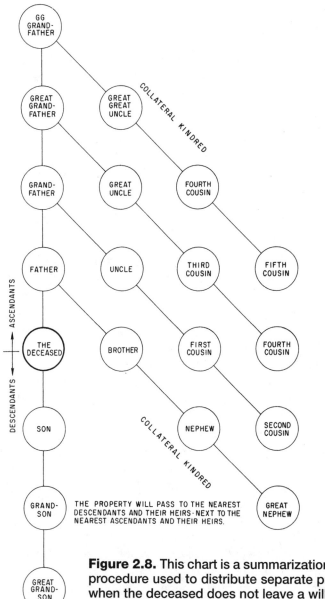

Figure 2.8. This chart is a summarization of the procedure used to distribute separate property when the deceased does not leave a will and is not survived by a husband or wife.

(text continued from page 49)

to the grandfather and grandmother in equal portions, but if only one of these is living, then this portion of the estate is again divided into two equal portions, one of which passes to the grandparent who is living, and the other passes to the descendant or descendants of the deceased grandparent. If the deceased grandparent has no descendants, then the portion of the estate that would have passed to that grandparent passes to the other grandparent who does survive; if there is no grandfather or grandmother surviving, then the estate passes to their descendants, "and so on without end, passing in like manner to the nearest lineal ancestors and their descendants." If there are no relatives at all, the property "escheats" (passes) to the State of Texas.

2. *If the Intestate Leaves a Husband or Wife.* (a) If the intestate leaves a husband or wife, then his estate (his separate estate) will pass and be inherited as follows (Figure 2.9): one-third of the personal property (movable property, money in bank, livestock, vehicles, corporate stocks, bonds, etc.) to his surviving wife and two-thirds to his children and their descendants, if he has a deceased child or children survived by descendants; and the homestead and one-third of his other real property (lands, minerals in the land, and houses) to his surviving wife as a life estate to be used and enjoyed by her during her lifetime with the remainder passing after her death to his children and their descendants along with the other two-thirds interest in the real property; (b) if the intestate has no child or children, or their descendants, the surviving spouse (Figure 2.10) will inherit all of the personal property and one-half of the real property, without remainder to anyone else with right to sell it or to pass it by will, and the other one-half of the real property passes according to the laws of descent and distribution to the kindred of the deceased; provided, however, that if the deceased has neither father nor mother nor any brother or sis-

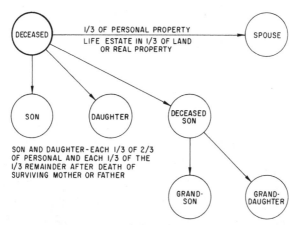

Figure 2.9. Distribution of separate property when the deceased does not leave a will but is survived by a husband or wife.

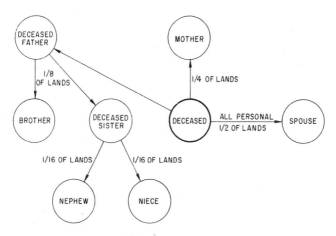

Figure 2.10. In the distribution of separate property when the deceased does not leave a will and is survived by husband or wife, but there are no children of the deceased nor their descendants and no father nor mother nor their descendants, the surviving spouse will take the whole estate in fee.

ter, or their descendants, the surviving spouse will receive and inherit the whole estate of the deceased spouse.

Note that these illustrations deal only with the separate property of the deceased—not with community property.

Community Estate

The community estate is owned in equal shares by the husband and wife. When one of them dies, the survivor's one-half of the community estate is not affected, and the survivor will inherit the deceased's half of the community property if there are no children of the deceased or their descendants. In 1993, the Probate Code was amended to give all community property to the surviving spouse, if all the surviving children are also the children of the surviving spouse. If the child is not a child of the surviving spouse, that child will receive one-half of the community property that would otherwise go entirely to the surviving spouse.

Passage of property by inheritance can be better understood if one keeps in mind that kinship derives from a common ancestor or ancestors. For example, first cousins are relatives because they have the same grandparents. Brothers are related to each other because they have the same parents. A person is related to his uncle because his grandparents are the uncle's parents.

Inheritance *per capita* instead of *per stirpes* occurs when a person dies intestate leaving as his only heirs relatives of the same class relation to him (Fig. 2.11). It is rather unusual but it does sometimes happen. If the deceased leaves heirs that are related to him in different degrees of kinship, then the rule will not apply, and the inheritance will be *per stirpes*.

Sometimes a will provides that certain beneficiaries will take "*per capita* and not *per stirpes*," or vice versa. If they take *per stirpes*, this means the beneficiaries take only that share of the

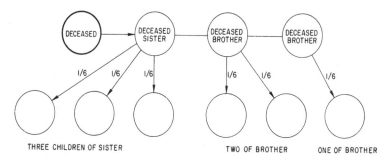

Figure 2.11. Inheritance *per capita* instead of *per stirpes*, which is rather unusual, means that if a man dies intestate, leaving no wife surviving him, and no children or their descendants, and his parents are deceased, and his sister and two brothers are deceased, but they are each survived by children, the children will be given equal shares because they are all the same class relation to the deceased.

estate their ancestor would have received. In a *per capita* distribution, all heirs of the same degree of kinship share equally. For example, Grandfather Bill has three sons: James, Robert, and Joe. Grandfather Bill wills his estate to his sons in equal shares, but he outlives all three. James is survived by one daughter, Robert by two sons, and Joe by 10 sons and daughters. In a *per stirpes* distribution, James' daughter gets all of his share of Grandfather Bill's estate, but Joe's 10 children divide up Joe's share between them. In a *per capita* distribution, the grandchildren get equal shares.

Matters Affecting and Not Affecting the Right to Inherit

Persons Not in Being. If a child of an intestate is born to the surviving wife after his death, that child will inherit from the father the same as if it had been born before the father's death.

Such a child would also be entitled to participate in the father's estate if the father should leave a valid will in which he provides benefits for his other children. In this case, the child born after his father's death would by law participate on an equal basis with the other children.

Heirs of Whole and Half Blood. When a person dies intestate and his property is inherited by his collateral kindred (which would be the case if he had no children, no wife, no father nor mother, nor other ascendants or descendants in the direct line), those of the half blood will inherit only half as much as those of the whole blood of the same class. For example, a half-brother or half-sister would inherit only half as much as a whole-brother or whole-sister. If all of those inheriting should be of the half blood, however, they would inherit whole parts.

Aliens. By provision of our constitution and statutes, aliens can inherit property in Texas.

Convicted Persons and Suicides. It does not matter that a person may have been convicted of a crime, he can inherit from his kindred and they can inherit from him, and the estates of those who die intestate by taking their own lives will pass and be inherited the same as if they had met natural deaths. Under provisions of the Insurance Code, however, if a person who is a beneficiary under a life insurance policy intentionally causes the death of the insured, he forfeits his right to receive the benefits of the policy. The benefits would go to the next of kin of the insured.

Inheritance Rights of Biological Children. In 1989, the legislature removed from the Probate Code references to children as "legitimate" and "illegitimate." A biological child has the same rights of inheritance as other children "with respect to its mother and its mother's kindred." It can inherit from her and them, and she and her kindred can inherit from the child. It is considered a child also for the purpose of determining homestead rights. A mother living in her homestead with her biological child has the same exemptions from forced sale (foreclosure by creditors) that she would have if the child had been born in lawful wedlock.

Advancement Brought into Hotchpotch. It so often happens that a father or mother will advance to one of the children (give to that one out of his or her estate) a portion of the family fortune or accumulation, and later when the parent dies intestate the child who received the gift or advancement comes forward for a portion of the intestate's remaining estate. If the child who received the gift or advancement brings back the amount he received so that it can be added back to the intestate's estate and can be distributed to the children along with the other assets, there can be no question about that child's right to participate in the distribution of the estate. It may be that he received a tract of land as an advancement and then sold it so that he cannot return that particular tract of land; however, it suffices if he returns, or "brings into hotchpotch," the value of the advancement. In bringing an advancement back into hotchpotch, it is not necessary that the money or other thing of value be physically returned. The value of the advancement can be added to the sum total of the intestate's estate, and when the division is made the value of the advancement can be subtracted from the amount awarded to the child who received the advancement.

Now, there is no difficulty when the one receiving the gift or advancement treats it as an "advancement." The law, however, provides that "every gratuitous *inter vivos* transfer is deemed to be an absolute gift and not an advancement unless proved to be an advancement." So here there is some difficulty when the child who received a gift or advancement contends that it was a gift and insists that he should share in the remaining estate on an equal basis with the other children. He has the law in his favor, and the burden is upon the other children to refute the legal presumption. If they fail to prove that it was in fact an advancement, intended by the parent to be an advancement to the child out of his future inheritance, then the child who received it can retain the gift and also participate with the other children in equal shares of the intestate's remaining estate.

The choice lies mainly with the one receiving the gift or advancement. Under any circumstance, he can keep the gift or advancement, whichever it may be, if he considers it more valuable than a further share in the intestate's estate. But if in fact it is proved to be an advancement and not an outright gift, the one who received it cannot keep it and also participate in the distribution of the remaining assets of the intestate's estate.

Passage of Title Upon Simultaneous Death. Frequently, in the case of deaths in fires, automobile accidents, plane crashes, and storms, there are questions arising as to which person survived the other. This is important because the time of death of the persons involved will often determine the course an inheritance will take. An interesting example is where a man and his wife who own a considerable community estate are both killed in an automobile accident and are not survived by any child or children or their descendants. Texas law provides that a person who fails to survive the decedent by 120 hours (or five days) is treated as if he predeceased the decedent. This is to avoid the situation where the passage of the entire estate would be determined by who died first—even by minutes. If it could be proved that the husband died first, then the whole of the community estate would pass to and be inherited by the wife's kindred. If it could be proved that the wife died first, then the whole of the community estate would pass to and be inherited by the husband's kindred.

If, in such deaths resulting from a common accident, it develops that neither spouse survived the other for 120 hours, the law provides that the estate will be inherited in equal shares by the kindred of the wife and the kindred of the husband; that is, equal shares will pass to each group. But in such simultaneous deaths it may be that the property rights are not exactly equal. The husband or the wife may have separate property and the other may not. In this instance the law provides that for the purpose of their estates it shall be considered that each one survived the other, and this means that neither will inherit from the other, leaving each one's estate to pass to his or her other heirs.

Here is another impelling reason why people should make wills. An attorney drafting a will can anticipate such occasions and provide for them in the will.

Survival of Beneficiaries. The 120-hour rule applies to beneficiaries also. If property is disposed of so that the right of a beneficiary to have an interest therein is conditional upon his surviving another person and the two meet death from a common cause, the beneficiary will be treated as if he predeceased the testator if he does not survive the testator by at least 120 hours. This means that his heirs will not inherit the property.

But if property is given alternatively to one of two or more beneficiaries with the right of each being dependent upon his surviving the other or others, and they all meet death under circumstances so that it cannot be determined in which order they died, the property will be divided into as many equal portions as there are beneficiaries, and the heirs of each will inherit a portion.

Joint Owners. If stocks, bonds, money in bank, or other personal property is owned so that one of two persons will be entitled to it upon the death of the other and they both die under such circumstance that it cannot be determined which survived the other, the property will be divided into two equal parts and the heirs of each will inherit a part. If there are more than two persons owning the property, it will be divided into as many shares as there are owners, and the heirs of each owner will inherit a share.

Insured and Beneficiary. When the insured and the beneficiary under a life or accident policy meet death under such circumstances that it cannot be determined who died first, the proceeds of the policy will be distributed as if the insured had survived the beneficiary, meaning that the proceeds will pass to the estate of the insured and be inherited by his heirs or be distributed according to the terms of his will if he leaves a valid will.

If those dying under the circumstances mentioned above leave writings (contracts or wills) showing their intentions that their property not follow the courses provided by law, then the writings, if clearly understandable, will be effective instead of the applicable provision of the law.

Federal and State Taxes Upon Estates of Decedents

The United States government and the State of Texas impose a tax upon estates of decedents that are valued above the exemptions or credits allowed, and these taxes apply the same whether the decedent left a valid will or died intestate. Prior to January 1, 1977, the federal government allowed the first $60,000 of any decedent's estate to pass to the heirs or beneficiaries free of tax.

The Tax Reform Act of 1976 combined the federal estate and gift tax into one unified transfer tax. The cumulative total of transfers previously subject to the two taxes was subjected to a single progressive rate schedule. The effect of this on the estate of a person who died in 1981 would be to give a combined exemption of $175,000; that is, if the value of the estate (including gifts subject to the tax) was less than that amount, it would not be a taxable estate.

But even greater liberalization has come with the Economic Recovery Tax Act of 1981. The effect of this law is to exempt the estates of the great majority of Americans from any estate or gift tax. The act continues the unified transfer tax system begun in 1976, but increases the "exemption equivalent" from $175,000 to $600,000 by 1987. By 1987, there was no estate or gift tax on transfers totaling $600,000 or less. This exemption was increased again by Congress in 1997. Th exemption will eventually be $1,000,000, to be phased in over a 10-year period. At this writing, the exemption is $650,000 per individual.

It is necessary to file a federal return only if the gross estate of a decedent exceeds the listed "exemption equivalent" for the year of his death.

Prior to September 1981, there was a separate inheritance tax applicable to residents of Texas; it was based upon the amount received by each beneficiary. This was changed by the 1981 legislature. The statute now simply says that ". . . a tax equal to the amount of the federal credit is imposed on the transfer at death of the property of every resident." So the Texas estate tax is now tied to the federal tax; if there is no federal tax due, there obviously will be no Texas tax. In Texas, however, a return must be filed even if no tax is due.

The new federal legislation also provides for an unlimited marital deduction. This means if a husband leaves all of his estate to his surviving wife, or vice versa, there will be no state tax.

3. Property: Personal, Real, and Corporate

Americans traditionally are landowners. One of the first concerns of English colonists was to acquire land on which they could build homes. George Washington was a land surveyor and the owner of extensive lands centering around his impressive estate at Mount Vernon, Virginia. John Adams, the second president, was the son of a farmer. Thomas Jefferson, the third president, owned an estate called Monticello in Virginia, and surrounded his mansion with a complete farming domain. James Madison was the son of a planter. Andrew Jackson received much of his compensation for legal fees in land, and after serving as the seventh president, returned to his land near Nashville, Tennessee—his beloved Hermitage. Robert E. Lee, a great military leader, loved his native Virginia and his home, Arlington.

Incidents of Ownership of Land

Unlike many foreign countries, the United States government, along with the other states including the State of Texas, recognizes complete ownership of land. There are some limitations, but generally this means the owner of a tract of land owns the vegetation growing upon it, the water in its strata below the surface, and all minerals. Theoretically at least, this ownership goes to the center of the earth terminating at a mere point.

This ownership implies severability or the right to sell out of the land any or all of the minerals and other rights. So when one is acquiring land, he should find out what has been done by prior owners. A part or all of the minerals may have been sold by a prior owner; or an oil, gas, and mineral lease may have been sold; or timber on the land may have been sold and the purchaser is to remove it at a later date; or the fresh water rights have been sold. In all such instances, the one purchasing the land recognizes those prior severed and outstanding interests and is subject to them.

Land titles originate from what is commonly termed the "sovereignty of the soil." Before Texas became a state, it was an independent nation, the Republic of Texas. Before it was a republic, it was one of the states of Mexico, and was originally a possession of Spain.

Each of these sovereign powers, during its ownership of the land that is now Texas, was the "sovereignty of the soil" and could grant title to the land. Mexico, and Spain before it, in transferring the title to the land, did not part with the minerals. It was those governments' theory that the minerals belonged to the government and no minerals should be privately owned. Mexico presently claims title to minerals in all lands within its borders.

When Texas became independent of Mexico, it adopted the English rule, which considered minerals the property of the land owner. As a state, Texas has the same rule, and as a result, one who owns the land owns the minerals in it unless there has been a severance. Even the Spanish grants and the Mexican grants are considered by the State of Texas to have conveyed the minerals with the soil, even though those governments did not so intend it at the time the grants were made.

In 1897, however, the Texas Legislature passed a law that provided that thereafter sales should be without the minerals, and from that date, purchasers acquiring lands from the state took the lands with the mineral rights reserved by the state. In these sales, there was a severance of all of the mineral rights from the soil.

In 1919, the legislature enacted the so-called "Relinquishment Act," which appointed the owner of the soil as the state's agent for leasing minerals in the land. For his services, the agent (the owner of the surface of the land) is given a share in the returns from the lease.

Land Grants from the Sovereignty

The first conveyance out of the sovereignty of the soil is generally referred to as a "grant." By scanning records in the various counties or those in the General Land Office in Austin, one will find that the Spanish government made many land grants before Mexico gained her independence from Spain, and many were made by the Government of Mexico before Texas gained her independence from Mexico. Likewise, the Republic of Texas continued to make land grants, and Texas still follows the practice.

It may seem that these governments were extravagant in granting, in some instances, such large tracts of land to people who settled upon the soil or to people who had rendered military or other service to the sovereign. The large grants can be accounted for by understanding that these several governments were anxious to have people settle upon the land and make it productive and thereby create wealth. Moreover, the governments desired to give people title to the land so it could be taxed and bring in revenue for support of the government.

The Original Survey or Measurement of the Land

It was the practice of these early governments to require the owner of the land grant to have the land surveyed at his own expense. Of course, in the early days few people were qualified to make accurate land surveys, and often a person who knew very little about surveying would be designated as the public or official surveyor in a colony. It is probable that some of them did not possess surveying instruments. Moreover, there were no roads leading to the lands they were to survey, and transportation was slow and difficult. So it could be expected that some surveys would be inaccurate, some of them so much so that the poorly delineated lines could not be followed, or not any or only some of the corners could be found. But people moved in and occupied the land and it was not the government's policy to move them out because of the inaccuracy of the land survey. Even after Texas became a state, the legislature passed acts intended to validate all of these Spanish, Mexican, and Republic of Texas land grants.

Despite all of this, some of these old surveys have been challenged, but even with the inaccuracies they have been hard to invalidate. Even the State of Texas has filed proceedings against some of the old titleholders, mainly on the grounds that outlines of a survey include more land than the grant specified. It is only reasonable to expect that those first surveyors would be generous with the person applying for the land since he was paying them for their work. Because of the surveyors' generosity, most of these old surveys contained more, rather than less, land than the grant specified.

In one instance where the state sued, the excess land mapped out by the surveyor amounted to 11 leagues. A league is 4,428 acres of land, and 11 leagues amount to a sizable pasture—48,708 acres. Regardless of this excess, the courts supported those claiming the land under the grant. It is a rule in Texas that if the surveyor's footsteps can be traced and the corners he described and designated can be found, the survey cannot be defeated because of excess land within its outlines, even 11 leagues of excess land. It is often jocularly said that those frontier surveyors measured the land with a coonskin and threw in the tail for good measure.

Land Deeds

Voluntary conveyances of land, after the original grant, are made by deeds. A deed properly made is a written instrument reciting a consideration, containing words of grant, describing the land conveyed so that it can be located, and generally containing some warranty (or guarantee) of title. They fall into three general classes:

The general warranty deed. The grantor agrees to defend the title that is given to the grantee, his heirs, executors, administrators, successors, and assigns against all persons who may claim it against them. In it, he even binds his executors and administrators to do so. In this situation, if the title fails, the grantor can be sued for the loss suffered by the purchaser.

The special warranty deed. The grantor warrants the title only against those who may claim it by, through, or under him. He does not guarantee that the title is good against any and all persons who may later claim it, but he does guarantee that he, himself, has not sold or encumbered the land.

The quit claim deed. The grantor does not guarantee or warrant anything. He does not even claim that he has the title, but in effect, he says such title that he has, he hereby conveys. If the title fails, he is not responsible.

There is also another kind of deed sometimes used that is a different version of the quit claim deed. It is one in which the grantor, where the warranty clause would ordinarily be written, finishes it with, "but this conveyance is without warranty of title," or other words to that effect. Here again, the grantor frees himself of responsibility if the title fails.

Necessity for Title Examination or Title Insurance

When one is purchasing land, it is necessary that he assure himself that he is getting a good title. It is not sufficient that the man or the company selling him the land warrants the title. The one who sells the land may not be financially responsible or may not continue to be financially responsible so that a loss could be recovered against him. There are two general methods commonly used, and they are both effective in assuring the purchaser that he is receiving good title.

In the first method, the purchaser may require of the seller that he furnish a complete abstract of title. This is supplied by an abstracter, generally a corporation chartered for the purpose and under bond to guarantee the accuracy of its work. The abstract is a compilation of all of the deeds and other records in the county in which the land is located that affect, or have any bearing on, the title to the land involved. It will contain a copy of all of those documents and constitutes a complete history of the title to the land. With this abstract, the purchaser, before he pays the consideration or becomes obligated for it, places it with his attorney for examination. The attorney will review the title's whole history and give a written opinion to the purchaser. If the attorney shows or states in his opinion that the purchaser will be receiving a good title by the proposed deed from the seller, or that the seller has good title at the time the abstract is closed, then the purchaser can depend upon that opinion and close the trade.

In the second, the purchaser may require that the seller furnish a guaranteed title, or title insurance, by a title insurance or title guaranty company. This title policy, or title insurance policy, should be delivered to the purchaser's attorney so he can make sure that the "exceptions" that may be contained in it do not leave too much risk for the purchaser to bear. If the purchaser's attorney states that the title insurance is in order, and that the purchaser is properly protected, then the purchaser can feel confident that he is receiving a good title by the deed from the seller.

In each of these instances, it should be kept in mind that the warranty in the deed and the title insurance protect the purchaser against loss only to the extent of the land's purchase price. One might think that, if he purchases a tract of land for $1,000 and has a general warranty in his deed or has title insurance and the land later is worth $10,000 and the title fails, he would be entitled to recover under the warranty or the insurance policy the current land value ($10,000). That is not the rule. He would only be able to recover the purchase price.

Both of these methods are extensively used, and a purchaser should be governed by his attorney's advice as to which one he chooses.

Necessity for Recording the Deed

As soon as the transaction is closed, the purchaser should place his deed of record in the county clerk's office in the county where the land is located. If the transaction is handled by a title insurance company or title guaranty company, that company will record the deed. When the deed is recorded, it is notice that the land described in the deed belongs to the person named as the purchaser, and all persons having any dealings pertaining to that tract of land are bound by the notice given by the recording of the deed.

If the purchaser fails to record his deed, he is subject to risks from different directions:

1. The seller might forget that he has sold the land and sell it to someone else who does not know about the previous sale, and, in this case, the second purchaser, if he is truly an innocent purchaser, will own the land.
2. The seller might forget that he has sold the land and borrow money and give a mortgage on the land to secure the loan, in which case, if the loan is not paid, the lender of the money might foreclose his mortgage and the first purchaser would lose his title to the land.
3. The seller might be sued for some other obligation and a judgment against him would create a lien against the land, and the purchaser may then lose the land.

There are other reasons why a deed should be recorded, but those listed are sufficient to show that a purchaser should lose no time in getting his deed of record.

Vendor's Lien

In the sale of land, more often than otherwise, part of the consideration is paid in cash and the balance of it is represented by promissory vendor's lien notes to be paid at later specified dates. The deed, by which title is conveyed, states the amount to be paid and describes briefly the notes that are signed by the purchaser, and it stipulates that a vendor's lien is retained to secure payment of the notes, the interest, and attorney fees, if placed with an attorney for collection. It often also mentions that the notes are further secured by a deed of trust executed by the purchaser to a named trustee.

The Deed of Trust

In the sale of real property—i.e., land, buildings, etc.—the usual procedure is for the seller to give the purchaser a deed, which is generally a warranty deed (but not always so) reciting the consideration paid and agreed to be paid by the purchaser for the property. The purchaser receives the deed from the seller and at the same time pays the cash consideration, which is only part of the total consideration.

The purchaser also signs vendor's lien notes to the seller to evidence the deferred payments to be made. At the same time, he signs a deed of trust to a trustee who is chosen by the seller. By this deed of trust, the purchaser conveys the title to the land to the trustee. This transferring of the title, however, is in trust to secure the payment of the notes, that are also described in the deed of trust, and conditioned so that if the notes are paid as they become due, the deed of trust will be of no further force and effect. This means that the title will then be the purchaser's by virtue of the deed from the seller, and not kept by the trustee. To clear his title of record, the purchaser must obtain from the seller a release of the vendor's lien and the deed of trust lien, and this instrument should be placed on record in the county clerk's office.

But if the purchaser fails to pay the notes, or any of them as they become due, the seller will call upon the trustee to sell the property at public auction in accordance with the authority granted to him in the deed of trust and apply the proceeds to the payment of the notes.

The particular virtue of the deed of trust is that the seller does not have to go to court to prove that default has been made in payment of the notes. The trustee has full authority, within the limits in the deed of trust, to post notices of sale and actually sell the property as a protection to the seller's interests. In addition to posting notices, the trustee shall give notice by certified mail to the debtor, by mailing it to his last known address. Of course, this must not be done wrongly or unjustly. The trustee is not authorized to make the sale unless the purchaser is actually in default, and it is very seldom that this mistake is made.

If there is a default, and the property is sold by the trustee, anyone may go to the sale and bid on the property. The successful bidder must pay cash for the property, and the trustee will deed the property to him. The trustee then pays the notes, if he receives enough money at the sale to do so, and, if there is any money left over, he pays it to the man who made the notes. If the amount received is insufficient to pay the full amount of the notes and the interest, he applies it as far as it will go, and then the seller may sue the maker for the balance due on the notes. The notes constitute a personal obligation of the maker, and he has no escape if what is received at the trustee's sale is inadequate.

Enforcing the Vendor's Lien Without the Deed of Trust

If the sale of the land is made for part cash and part vendor's lien notes, and no deed of trust is executed by the purchaser, as mentioned previously, then the enforcement of the vendor's lien necessitates court action. The holder of the notes cannot of his own volition take over the property or sell it at public auction, as the trustee in the deed of trust could do when a deed of trust is used. The one holding the defaulted notes must bring a suit in the district court, since it involves title to land, and he must prove to the court's satisfaction that he is the owner of the notes or note on which he sues, that default has been made, that he has demanded payment and that payment has not been made, and that the amount he sues for is still due and unpaid.

If the court is satisfied with the proof offered, a judgment will be entered against the maker of the notes for the principal sum due, the interest, and the attorney's fee. This judgment itself will constitute a lien against the land in favor of the plaintiff (the one who brings the suit). In due time, an execution will be issued by the court clerk directing the county sheriff, in which the land is located, to levy upon the property and to sell it at public auction.

Due notice of sale will be given, and at the courthouse door on the appointed date, the sheriff will offer the land for sale and will sell it to the highest bidder for cash. The sheriff will make the purchaser at the sale a deed to the land, and he will apply the proceeds to payment of the note or notes and the interest after deducting the court costs and his fees.

If the proceeds of the sale are sufficient to defray the expenses, the note or notes, interest, and the attorney fees, then the purchaser will owe no more, but he has lost his land. If the sale's proceeds are insufficient to satisfy the judgment in its entirety, the deficiency will stand as a remaining amount due on the judgment or as a deficiency judgment against the maker of the notes, and he may be faced with a levy upon and sale of other property to satisfy it.

Ownership of Land in Indivision—Partition

Frequently, several people acquire title to a tract of land so that each owns a fractional interest in it. This often results from inheritance; for example, one owning land may die intestate leaving several lawful heirs, which results in the heirs owning the land in indivision. Under certain circumstances, it may be desirable to continue to own the land in indivision, but generally, the owners will ultimately want their respective shares given to them separately so that each one will own a separate piece of acreage.

If there are only two people owning the land in indivision, the partition of it between them should be simple, but it is not always so. It has been suggested that the one desiring to divide the land should draw a plat and cut the land into two parts and let the other owner choose his half. If there are more than two owners, the problem is not so easy, and the greater the number of owners, the more difficult the problem becomes. If the owners can all agree, however, the land can be cut into as many parcels as there are owners, with all parcels having equal value, as near as may be reasonably determined, and a drawing is held so that each will receive a share, and all parties can enter into a partition deed to carry the drawing into effect.

But if no agreement on the method of division can be reached, the person or the persons desiring to divide the property can bring a suit for partition in the district court. No one is obligated to leave his land in indivision if he desires to have it partitioned.

It sometimes is desirable to leave the minerals in indivision, particularly if a portion of the land is in production. It has happened that a family will partition inherited land, minerals and all, and later find that one or more of the partitioned tracts produce oil or gas and the others do not. Again if the several owners are agreeable, however, they may partition the land, minerals and all, and then join together in making oil, gas, and mineral leases, all of them signing the same lease and describing all of the land in the lease. This is particularly desirable in the case of small tracts, say 5, 10, 15, or 20 acres each.

Thus, they pool and unitize their land for the purpose of the lease so that if oil or gas is discovered on any part of the land, they all will receive a royalty according to the amount of acreage owned, regardless of on whose tract the well may be located. After the lease is terminated, whether the land was productive or not before the lease's termination, the land is no longer pooled.

Of course, under the pooling provisions contained in most oil, gas, and mineral leases, the same thing can be accomplished. But if the owners of the several tracts make separate leases, it is the lessee who decides how the tracts are to be unitized. If the landowners join in one lease, however, they can also provide that if any part of the larger tract is put into a unit, the whole tract must be included. But even if they do not make such a provision and only part of the land is included in a producing unit, then all of the landowners will participate in the returns from that part that does go into the unit.

Minerals in the Land

Under our American ownership system, the minerals in the land belong to the landowner, unless the rights have been transferred or otherwise severed from the land. Minerals are considered part of the land or realty. This is different from the rules in many foreign countries where the minerals belong to the government, not to the individual who owns the land.

But minerals, which include oil and gas, can be sold out of the land or severed from it in whole or in part, even as a landowner may sell an undivided interest in his land itself. When one sells a tract of land without reserving the minerals, he or she sells the minerals with the land, even though no mention is made of minerals in the land deed.

The minerals in Texas land that are most valuable in the aggregate and most traded are oil, gas, and sulfur. Most of the sulfur found in this state is in the cap rock of salt domes. Oil and gas are found in porous formations in the earth, such as sand strata, porous limestone, cap rock of salt domes, etc.

Since the oil and gas industry has never been able to develop oil and gas finding techniques into an exact science, much of the land in Texas has potential value for oil and gas leasing; or oil, gas, and sulfur leasing; or oil, gas, and mineral leasing; even though it may never produce.

The oil, gas, and mineral lease is the document most commonly used when a landowner sells to the one buying the lease a right to explore his land for minerals, develop them, and market them. Usually the lease reserves for the landowner, or mineral owner, a portion of the minerals that may be found, produced, and marketed, and this retained or reserved interest is known as a "royalty." It is usually one-eighth of the oil and gas, free of cost, into the pipeline, and one dollar or more per long ton of sulfur mined and marketed. While the royalty on oil and gas is usually one-eighth, it may be more or less, according to the trade made between the landowner and the one buying the lease.

Also, the lease has a "primary term," say five years, during which the lease can be kept effective by paying annual rentals, and the lease will name a bank as the land or mineral owner's agent to receive the rentals. At the end of the primary terms, the one buying the lease will lose the lease unless he is then producing oil, gas, or other minerals from the land or carrying on operations upon the land for that purpose.

If oil, gas, or other minerals are produced upon the land during the primary term, then no delay rentals are necessary to keep the lease effective as long as production continues. Production will keep the lease effective as long as it continues after the end of the primary term, even though production began after the end of the lease's primary term but was a result of operations started on or before the end of the primary term and continued until production began.

There are many different forms of oil, gas, and mineral leases commonly used. Most major oil companies have their own forms that they prefer to use, and they differ from company to company in some respects, sometimes only in minor detail. But the leases generally follow a common pattern such as the form one can buy at stationery stores.

Royalty is Free of Production Costs

The royalty reserved under the lease's terms is produced into the tanks or into the pipeline to which the wells may be connected free of the production costs, but not tax free.

Pooling and Unitization

Most modern lease forms provide for the pooling or unitization of the land covered by the lease with other lands or leases in the immediate vicinity. This enables the operator of the leases to form units of more or less uniform size so that the oil in the pool, or common reservoir, can be produced without drilling excess wells. It also enables the operator to do a better job for the royalty owners.

By pooling and unitizing, the operator can come nearest to delivering to each royalty owner shares in the royalty oil and gas produced on the basis of the amount of royalty interest he owns in the pooled unit. To illustrate: If A owns 80 acres of land which he has leased with pooling privileges, and the operator forms a 160-acre unit by putting A's 80 acres in with another tract of 80 acres, then A will own one-half of his original fraction of royalty, but he will have it under a tract twice the size of his original tract. If he has a one-eighth royalty under his 80 acres, then he will have a one-sixteenth royalty under the 160-acre unit. With such a unit, it does not make any difference to A whether the well is drilled on his 80 acres or on the other half of the unit. He participates in the royalty just the same.

Overriding Royalty

The royalty reserved in an oil, gas, and mineral lease by a land or mineral owner is commonly called "base royalty," but there is another kind of royalty often created called "overriding royalty." If the lease holder sells the lease to another operator for the purpose of exploration and/or drilling, he most likely will reserve a fractional interest in the oil, gas, and other minerals (say one-thirty-second) in the assignment wherein he specifies that such royalty be paid or delivered to him free of the production cost. This is overriding royalty. The operator holding a lease may sell a fractional part of the oil, gas, and other minerals to be produced under terms of the lease and specify that such fractional part shall be paid to or delivered to the purchaser free of the production cost. In this case, he has sold an overriding royalty that he has carved out of his working interest.

When Minerals are Severed From the Land

Sometimes all of the minerals are sold out of the land, or a landowner may sell the land and reserve all of the mineral rights. If this happens, the one who owns the minerals has the same rights with respect to the minerals as he would have if he owned the land with the minerals. He can sell part or all of the minerals, carve out and sell royalty interests in the minerals, or he can lease the land for oil, gas, and mineral development.

The one who owns the land without owning any interest in the minerals cannot prevent the mineral-interest owner or the one who leased the rights from coming upon the land to develop the mineral estate. One acquiring a lease from the mineral-interest owner has the same rights that he would have if the minerals had not been severed from the land. If he does not do the land any more damage in his operations than is reasonably necessary, he will not owe the land owner any damages for his operations.

The one who owns the land without interest in the minerals is compensated by the lower price that he had to pay for the land, and he is charged with full knowledge when he buys the land that mineral production operations may be carried on upon the land to his inconvenience and to reasonable damage to the land.

Damages to Fences, Crops, and Timber upon the Land

Most oil, gas, and mineral leases provide that the one buying the lease will be responsible for damages to fences, growing crops, and timber upon the land caused by his operations. But even if a lease does not include this provision, the one who carries on such operations and causes damage will be responsible to the owner. It has been held repeatedly by the courts that an oil operator holding a valid oil and gas lease, or oil, gas, and mineral lease, has the right to use as much of the surface of the land and a roadway into the location as is necessary to his operation.

Controversies more often arise when the landowner leases his land for oil, gas, and other minerals, and, either before or afterward, leases the same land to another for agricultural purposes. The responsibility of the oil operator is little changed because of the agricultural lease. The tenant farmer is inclined to be far less tolerant toward the oil operator because he, the tenant farmer, will not benefit from the possible results from the operations in developing the minerals.

If the operator of an oil, gas, and mineral lease goes upon agricultural land when no crops are growing upon it, as in the wintertime, then he does not damage any growing crops in his operations. This is a different situation than going in the middle of a field with growing crops, making a road and occupying two or three acres for the drill site. On the other hand, if the operator goes on the land when there are no crops growing, then spring comes and the tenant farmer gets ready to plant, especially if the agricultural lease is older than the oil lease, the tenant farmer has a valid complaint that the landowner and the operator must answer.

Railroad Commission Regulation of Oil and Gas

Under Texas laws, the Railroad Commission is charged with regulating the oil and gas business in the state in its several phases—production, transportation, refining, and marketing. Before any well can be drilled in search of oil and gas, a permit must be obtained from the oil and gas division of the Railroad Commission, and that permit is for a specific location that cannot be changed without the commission's permission.

The permit is granted without charge to the applicant when the application is in order and shows the proposed location to be "regular," which is not requiring exception to the spacing or other rules of the commission. Every permit, however, requires the applicant to contact the Water Development Board and receive a direction as to the amount of surface casing required to protect the freshwater sands from pollution. Once the permit is issued and the applicant begins his operations, then he must make the following reports to the commission:

(a) A completion report to show how the well was completed, a dry hole or a producer, including a driller's log of the well to show the various strata or formations encountered in the drilling process;

(b) If the well is a dry hole, a plugging record must be furnished to show how the well was plugged. The rules require that the well be filled with mud and that it have cement plugs at such depths as will prevent the flow of saltwater into freshwater zones and prevent the escape of fluid from the well onto the surface of the ground;

(c) If the well is a producer, then a potential test must be made and reported to show how much oil or gas the well is capable of producing; and

(d) A report must be made to show the oil or gas purchasers whom the operator has authorized to receive the production from the well, and before these purchasers can move such products from the lease, they must have written authorization from the Railroad Commission.

Each month after the well is put on production, the operator must make a report to the Railroad Commission showing the amount of production from the well during the preceding month, the amount sold during the month, and the amount on hand in stock tanks at the end of the month. Heavy penalties are assessed on those making false reports.

A barrel of oil is defined by statute as 42 gallons, and a cubic foot of gas is defined as that amount of gas necessary to fill one cubic foot of space with a standard pressure of 14.65 pounds per square inch (which is atmospheric pressure at sea-level) at a standard temperature of 60 degrees Fahrenheit.

Eminent Domain

It is recognized by the laws of the State of Texas that it is necessary for the state or U.S. Government or their subdivisions to build public roads, streets, courthouses, libraries, post offices, military installations, public schools, water works, sewers, and other structures for the public good. It is also recognized that railroads, telephone and telegraph lines, and pipelines for gas or oil transportation or other products are necessary for all of the people, and therefore the right of "eminent domain" is an unusual power available to acquire real estate at a fair cost for building or construction of these necessities. Otherwise, general progress may be blocked to the injury of all. This is a case where individual rights must be subordinated to the public interest. Private owners whose property is taken in this manner, or "condemned," however, must be fairly and adequately compensated—a protection which is guaranteed to the property owner by Section 17, Article I of the *Texas Constitution*, under the "Bill of Rights."

If the government, its subdivision, a corporation, or any other entity having the right of eminent domain fails to make a settlement with the owner of needed real estate, a petition can be filed in the proper court in the county where the property is located. The petition must describe the property to be condemned, state the intended purpose, state the name of the owner, and allege that the entity and owner are unable to agree on damages. The petition must be filed in a county court at law or a district court. The judge will then appoint three "disinterested freeholders" as special commissioners.

These commissioners then, after giving the interested parties notice of the time and place, hold a hearing where both parties have the right to be heard and present evidence as to the value of the property to be taken, the resulting damage to other property, if any, of the owner or the value increase of the property, if any, which reasonably could be expected to result from the intended use of the property. The commissioners must make a statement in writing to the county judge based upon the evidence given at the hearing.

The notices for such a hearing must be served upon the interested parties not later than the eleventh day before the day set for the hearing, and the hearing must be at a convenient place near the property in question or at the county seat. The person serving the notices of hearing is generally the county sheriff, his deputy, or a constable, but any person qualified to testify may serve and return the notices.

The commissioners' report to the county judge shall give the damages they assessed to be paid by the party who is taking the property and the costs that have accrued in the proceedings and the party or parties on whom the costs shall fall, including a nominal fee for each commissioner for each day the commissioners have served.

If either party is dissatisfied with the decision, the party may, on or before the first Monday following the expiration of 20 days after the decision has been filed with the county judge, file his objections in writing, giving his grounds of objection. The adverse party shall be cited, and the cause shall be tried and determined as in other civil cases in the county court.

If no objections to the decision are filed, the judge will have the decision recorded in the minutes of the court, will make the decision the judgment of the court, and will issue necessary orders for its enforcement.

An appeal from the judgment of the court may be taken as in other civil cases. If the appeal is by the state or federal government or some subdivision of either, no appeal bond is to be posted by the appellant. If the appeal is by a private citizen or anyone else, not the state or federal government or their subdivisions, a bond is required. If an appeal is taken, however, the court's judgment is not suspended. Of course, if the appellate court makes a different decision from that of the lower court, the appellate court's decision and judgment will become effective and set aside the lower court's judgment.

On appeal, the losing party pays the court costs. For example, if a railroad company wants to condemn a piece of land belonging to a person to be used as a railroad station site and obtains judgment in the county court for possession of the land and in the judgment the price of the land is fixed, should the property owner be dissatisfied because the price is too low, he can appeal the case and on appeal he can obtain a judgment for a higher price than was fixed by county court. Then the railroad company will have to pay the court costs. If on appeal, however, the property owner does not obtain judgment for a higher price, he must pay the costs.

In condemnation proceedings under the right of eminent domain, the one condemning the property does not obtain the fee title to the property condemned. He obtains the use of the property only to serve the purpose he claims is the reason he needs the property. To illustrate, if a pipeline company brings an action under the right of eminent domain to build and operate a pipeline across A's land, and the company obtains judgment giving it the right to do so, the company does not acquire the fee title to the land, the title to the minerals in the land, or the grazing rights. The only right acquired is to build and operate a pipeline over and across the land. A still owns the land, but his use of it is subject to the right of the pipeline company to build and operate a pipeline. The pipeline company has an "easement."

The Law of Limitation

Actions for Land and the So-Called "Squatter's Rights"

"Limitation" as the word is used here means: (a) the time during which a person owning or claiming land has a right to commence a lawsuit to recover land in possession of another; and (b) the time that the one in possession must hold it adverse to the owner or claimant in order to perfect his title to it. If limitation (time) runs against the owner for sufficient time that he loses his title to the one in possession, then the owner has lost his title "by limitation," and the one in possession has perfected his title "by limitation." One who takes possession of land without the consent of the owner is commonly called a "squatter."

The statutes dealing with limitation describe the several different kinds: three, five, 10, and 25 years. The one we are most often confronted with is the ten-year limitation, and the article is quoted in full.

Ten Years' Possession

Section 16.026 of the Texas Civil Practice and Remedies Code states that:

(a) A person must bring suit not later than 10 years after the day the cause of action accrues to recover real property held in peaceable and adverse possession by another who cultivates, uses, or enjoys the property;

(b) Adverse possession is limited to 160 acres if there is no title instrument unless the number of acres actually enclosed exceeds 160; and

(c) Peaceable possession held under a registered memorandum of title other than a deed extends to the boundaries specified in the instrument.

Depending upon which side of the litigation a person may be on, this can be a very harsh rule. For instance, if a person has legitimate title to a piece of land and then finds that some other person has been living on it or using it as his own for 10 years, he then loses title to it. That is the way the law provides that the title can be passed. It is not necessary that the one in possession pay any taxes during the ten-year period, and the titleholder may himself be paying the taxes each year as they accrue.

Even under these circumstances, however, the titleholder can and will lose his title to the one living on his land if he does not bring suit within the ten-year period to oust the one in possession, if that one in possession uses the provisions of this article in his efforts to hold the land.

The person in possession, though, in order to perfect his title under this ten-year statute, must hold the land without the consent of the true owner. If he is in possession and using the land by the owner's permission, he is recognizing the owner's rights to the land, and this will defeat the possessor if he attempts to take the title. In order to perfect his title, the one in possession must at all times during the ten years treat the land as if it belonged to him and not at any time during such period recognize or acknowledge that the land belongs to anyone else.

Moreover, this man in possession of a portion of a large tract may, if he is well advised, perfect his title to 160 acres, even though he may have only a small portion of the land actually enclosed, by occupying it for 10 years. If he enclosed a tract larger than 160 acres and possesses it without the knowledge or consent of the record titleholder for 10 years, he perfects his title to the amount he has fenced.

Under this statute it is use and occupancy of the land for 10 years, at all times without recognizing the owner's rights, that perfects the title for the one in possession. He may pay taxes or he may not do so. The paying of taxes is not required under this statute for the one in possession to perfect his title.

Three Years' Possession

"A person must bring suit to recover real property held by another in peaceable and adverse possession under color of title not later than three years after the day the cause of action accrues." Sec. 16.024, *Texas Civil Practice and Remedies Code*

Title, as used in the foregoing article, is defined by statute as a regular chain of transfers from, or under, the sovereignty of the soil. By a regular chain, it is meant with none of the links missing. Color of title is defined as a consecutive chain of such transfers down to such person in possession, without being regular, as if one or more of the memorials or muniments are not registered, or not duly registered, or have some other irregularity; or when the party in possession shall hold the same by a certificate of headright, land warrant, or land scrip, with a chain of transfers down to him in possession. To hold the land under three years' possession, one must have something in the nature of record title.

Five Years' Possession

"(a) A person must bring suit not later than five years after the day the cause of action accrues to recover real property held in peaceable and adverse possession by another who:
    (1) cultivates, uses, or enjoys the property;
    (2) pays applicable taxes on the property;
    (3) claims the property under a duly registered deed.
(b) This section does not apply to a claim based on a forged deed or a deed executed under a forged power of attorney."
Sec. 16.025, *Texas Civil Practice and Remedies Code*

To perfect title under this statute, the one in possession must be able to prove:

(a) That he has been in peaceable and adverse possession of the land for a full five years;

(b) That he claims under a deed or deeds duly registered or recorded in the county in which the land is located and that his deed is not forged; and

(c) That he had paid the taxes currently each year, which means before they became delinquent.

There are conditions that will defeat one in possession in perfecting title by limitation or delay the starting of the limitation period, and examples are presented when the one owning the property is under some disability at the time the adverse possession starts, such as:

1. The owner of the land may be a minor, in which case the period of limitation will not start to run until the owner is no longer a minor.

2. The owner may be insane, in which case the limitation period will not start to run until the owner regains his sanity.

3. The owner may be serving a sentence in prison, in which case the limitation period will not start to run until his release therefrom.

4. The owner may be serving in the military service during war, in which case the limitation period would not start to run until the military service or the war ends.

The Twenty-Five Year Statute of Limitation

One holding possession of real estate, using and enjoying it continuously for 25 years, under a deed or deeds or other instruments that have been recorded in the deed records of the county in which the real estate is located, will thereby perfect his title regardless of whether the owner may be under some disability as mentioned under Conditions 1 through 4 previously stated.

Once the limitation period has started running in favor of the one in possession, with respect to any of the periods mentioned, the only thing that will stop it or interrupt it is a suit to remove the person in possession. If the person having the right to sue for removal of the one in possession delays bringing suit until the full period has run, whichever period it may be, then he has lost his right.

Moreover, the use and possession of the land does not have to be all by one person. One who takes possession adverse to the landowner may occupy it for a time and then deliver possession to another who continues to hold possession to the end of the period. The owner has then lost his title the same as if the same person had continued in possession, because under the law, the second one to hold can "tack" the time of his possession onto the time of the one before him. There must be privity of estate between them, however, which is agreement between them for the holding of the property.

Minerals in the Land under Adverse Possession

If the minerals in the land are intact, which means that they have not been severed or sold out of the land, then when the title to the land has been perfected by limitation it will include the minerals. But if the minerals have been severed from the land before the limitation period starts, then the minerals would not be included in the title to the land. The "squatter" would not get the minerals, unless, of course, he used the land in a way that would serve as notice that he was also claiming the minerals. He could do this by drilling for the minerals and producing them and continuing the appropriation during the full limitation period. If he did that without interruption, he would thereby acquire the minerals also, even though they had been previously severed from the land. This is not likely to happen, for the reason that one drilling for and producing oil, gas, or other minerals must show good title to the purchaser of such minerals before he can sell them, unless, of course, the producer of the minerals is the same one who refines and sells them.

Once the limitation period starts to run, severing the minerals during the period will not save them. It is necessary that a suit be brought for the purpose of ousting the "squatter" before the end of the period. Coverture (or marriage) does not prevent the running of limitation on land against a married woman.

Assignment for Creditors

Sometimes a man finds he is unable to pay his debts, and when this happens he may be forced into bankruptcy. However, if he still has enough assets so that when they are applied to his debts no creditor will receive less than one-third of his claim, he may be discharged from further liability to his creditors, without going through the delay and expense of a bankruptcy proceeding.

He accomplishes this by making an assignment for the benefit of his creditors. The assignment will include all of his property, except items exempt from forced sale. He will not be discharged from liability to any creditor who does not receive as much as one-third of the amount due and allowed in his favor as a valid claim against the debtor's estate. An assignment for the benefit of creditors is a voluntary transfer by a debtor of some or all of his property to an assignee, in trust, to be applied to the payment of some or all of the debts.

The assignment must be in writing, acknowledged, and recorded in the same manner provided by law for real estate conveyances. It must contain an inventory of debtor's property and it must include the following:

1. A list of all of the debtor's creditors;
2. The place of residence of each creditor, if known;
3. The sum owed each creditor, and the nature of the debt or demand;
4. The consideration of such indebtedness in each case, and the place where such indebtedness arose;
5. A statement of any existing judgment or security for the payment of any such debt; and
6. An inventory of all such debtor's estate at the date of such assignment, both real and personal, and any existing encumbrances, and all relative vouchers and securities and the value of the estate.

The person making the assignment must make a sworn statement to the truth of the assignment, which he must sign.

When the assignment is made, the assignee (the one receiving the assets from the debtor) gives notice of his appointment within 30 days by publishing the notice in a newspaper printed in the county where the assignor resides. If there is not a newspaper in the county, then the notice is printed in the newspaper nearest the place of business of the person making the assignment. This publication is to be continued once each week for three consecutive weeks. In addition, the assignee gives notices to each of the listed creditors by mail.

Acceptance by Creditors

The creditors of the one making the assignment who consent to the assignment must give notice to the assignee within four months after the assignee's notice is issued. A creditor who does not consent will not be entitled to any benefits under the assignment. A creditor who had no actual notice may consent to the assignment at any time before distribution of the assets, and he will thereby be entitled to his portion of the distribution. Any creditor who receives any portion of his claim from the assignee is presumed to agree to the assignment.

The assignee is required to give bond as fixed by the county or district judge binding him to a faithful discharge of his duties. Also, he must record the assignment in the county where he resides and in each county where any of the assigned property may be located. He is obligated to make distribution of the assigned property or to sell it and distribute the proceeds from the sale to the creditors according to the amounts of the claims filed and approved. If the assignee fails to act promptly as the law provides, he may be removed and may be replaced by another to act as assignee in his place.

Inasmuch as a creditor who does not agree to the assignment cannot receive any benefits under the assignment, and the one making the assignment must assign all of his property except that which is exempt from forced sale, it is wise for a creditor to accept it promptly; otherwise he will not be able to collect anything on his claim. A nonconsenting creditor, however, can force the petitioner into bankruptcy if he so desires.

Landlord and Tenant

A lease is a conveyance of an actual estate in land. It gives a right of possession to the tenant, to the exclusion of everyone including the landlord, except for the reasonable right of inspection and such other specific entry rights as the landlord may have reserved to himself in the lease. An oral lease agreement is just as binding as a written agreement unless it is for a term of more than one year, in which case there must be a writing to satisfy the Statute of Frauds.

Most people do not realize that the grant of the use of the land and the promise to pay rent are separate agreements. If the tenant fails to pay the rent, the landlord cannot evict him, unless there is an agreement in the lease giving him that power. Without such an agreement, the landlord's only remedy is to file suit for the back rent. This is not a practical problem, because virtually all lease agreements include such provisions.

Other agreements in the lease are normally considered to be independent covenants. For example, the landlord's duty to repair and the tenant's obligation to pay rent are independent; even though the landlord defaults in his promise to make repairs, the tenant is still obligated to pay the rent. If the failure to repair is serious enough, it may entitle the tenant to break the lease and move elsewhere, but this is his only remedy.

Notice for Terminating Tenancies

Where there is a written lease agreement, termination notice is controlled by the terms of the agreement. Where the lease is oral or there is no provision in the written lease, the type of notice is controlled by the frequency of rent payments. In a typical monthly tenancy or tenancy from month to month, there must be 30 days' notice. When the rent is paid at periods of less than a month, the time of notice of termination is sufficient if it is equal to the interval between the times of payment.

Subletting and Assignment

Many people believe that a tenant has the right to sublet or assign the leased premises unless the lease agreement contains a provision forbidding him to do so. The opposite is true. The Texas statutes deny a tenant this privilege, unless he has obtained the consent of the landlord to do so.

Liens to Secure Obligations

A lien is a security interest in property to secure a financial obligation. A party who holds a lien to secure a debt can hold the property if the debt is not paid. Landlords and tenants have liens against the property of the other in certain situations. If the tenant or his property is damaged because of the landlord's failure to comply with the lease agreement, the tenant has a lien on all of the property in his (tenant's) possession not exempt from forced sale, as well as rents due under the contract. While this law could give some leverage to farm tenants, it is of little practical value to modern urban apartment tenants.

The landlord also has a lien upon the property of the tenant located in the rented premises to secure rent that is due. This lien, however, can attach only to property that is not exempt from forced sale by the statutes of Texas. In addition, there is a landlord's lien that went into effect on September 1, 1973, for the benefit of the operator of any residential house, apartment, duplex, or other single- or multiple-family dwelling. The lien attaches to "all property found within the tenant's dwelling," except for specific items listed in the statutes. Interestingly, two very common household items are not included and are therefore subject to the lien: televisions and stereos.

Tenant Protection

Several statutes have been passed in recent years to give tenants greater legal protection, though Texas certainly does not go as far in this regard as many jurisdictions. It is now unlawful for a landlord to have a tenant's utilities cut off, where the tenant pays the utilities directly to the utility company. It is also unlawful for a landlord to willfully exclude a tenant from the rented premises in any manner except by judicial process. The same statute, however, gives the landlord the right to change the door locks "when the tenant's rents are in fact delinquent in whole or in part." The statute then provides that when this is done, a written notice shall be left on the tenant's front door describing where the new key may be obtained at any hour, and the name of the individual who will be there to provide it. The key must be provided regardless of whether the tenant pays any delinquent rents.

When the tenant has abandoned the premises, the landlord has the right to remove the contents.

Security Deposits

Another statute governs security deposits made by a tenant in residential property. It provides that within 30 days after the tenant moves out, he shall give the landlord notice of his new address, and during that time the landlord must return the security deposit. If the landlord withholds all or any part of the deposit, he must during this time return the balance of the deposit, if any, along with an itemized list and description of all damages and charges for which the tenant is liable and for which the landlord is deducting from the deposit. No deposit may be retained to cover "normal wear and tear." The landlord bears the burden of proving the reasonableness of these charges.

The landlord who in "bad faith" retains a security deposit without furnishing the itemized list is liable for $100 plus treble the amount wrongfully withheld from the tenant, plus attorney's fees. Failure to return the security deposit or itemized list creates a presumption of "bad faith" against the landlord. This is not true if the tenant fails to furnish the landlord his last known address.

Rights and Duties of Landlord and Tenant

In 1979, the Texas Legislature passed a statute attempting to further define the landlord-tenant relationship. It applies only to residential rental units.

The statute is long and complex. Among other things, it requires the landlord to make a diligent effort to repair or remedy "any condition which materially affects the physical health or safety of an ordinary tenant." This obligation is not incurred if the tenant is in arrears in his rent or has failed to give a reasonable notice of the condition in need of repair.

If the landlord fails to comply, the tenant has several remedies. He can terminate the tenant rental agreement and move, in which case he is entitled to a pro rata return of any rent he has paid for the current month or term, or he can file a lawsuit and obtain several possible remedies from the court, along with his attorney's fees.

Within six months of the tenant's repair notice, the landlord cannot take actions, such as filing a notice of eviction or decreasing services to the tenant, that can be interpreted as retaliation.

The tenant also can be guilty of retaliation if he, in response to the landlord's failure to repair, withholds rent due the landlord.

It is possible for these provisions to be waived in the rental agreement if the waiver is underlined or in bold print, or is in a separate written addendum.

The Statute of Frauds

This statute has a long history, going back to English jurisprudence. Its purpose was to prevent frauds, though it has at times been used to perpetrate frauds on the ill-informed. Under this statute, lawsuits cannot be brought in any state court to enforce certain agreements, unless the agreements or promises, or some memorandum thereof, are in writing and signed by the party to be charged or by some person authorized by him. These agreements include:

1. A suit to charge an executor or administrator upon any promise to answer any debt or damage due from his testator or intestate, out of his own estate;
2. A suit to charge any person upon a promise to answer for the debt, default, or miscarriage of another;
3. A suit based on an agreement made upon consideration of marriage or on consideration of nonmarital conjugal cohabitation;

4. A suit upon any contract for the sale of real estate, or upon any contract to lease real estate for a longer term than one year;

5. A suit upon lease of real estate for a term longer than one year;

6. A suit upon any agreement that is not to be performed within the time of one year from the making;

7. A suit for the collection of a commission for the sale or purchase of oil and/or gas minerals leases, oil and/or royalties, minerals or mineral interest, or a suit for commission for the sale of the land; and

8. A suit to enforce an agreement or warranty to cure by a physician or health care provider.

The last provision was not part of the original statute of frauds, but was passed with a package of laws in 1977 that were intended to give physicians greater protection from malpractice suits.

Although the statute of frauds is subject to abuse, it is generally believed that it prevents people from being subjected to much harassment and expense in defending themselves against claims that are not well-founded.

Conveyances to Defraud

The Fraudulent Transfer Act (Sec. 24.005) of the Texas Business and Commerce Code provides that a transfer made or obligation incurred by a debtor is fraudulent if made with the actual intent to hinder, delay, or defraud the creditor. It is fraudulent also if the debtor made the transfer without receiving reasonably equivalent value in exchange, and, when compared to the transaction, the remaining assets are "unreasonably small."

In determining actual intent, courts may look at such factors as whether the transfer was to an insider, whether the debtor retained actual possession of the property, whether the transfer was concealed, and other facts that would show an intent to avoid payment.

The act details other typical attempts of debtors to transfer property to avoid liabilities. It also provides remedies for defrauded creditors. A creditor can sue to set aside the transfer, attach the property in the hands of the purchaser, and ask for an injunction to prevent further transfers. A good faith purchaser, however, is protected if the purchaser bought the property in good faith and paid a "reasonably equivalent value" for the property.

Probably one of the most prevalent attempts to fraudulently convey is in the case where a property owner finds himself in financial difficulties with creditors and transfers the title of his property to a relative or close friend for no consideration of any value, or for a consideration far below the property value. The courts in well-presented cases have consistently held such conveyances void when used as attempts to evade creditors.

If a person conveys his property to another in an effort to hide it from creditors, the courts will not aid him in his effort to recover it, even though he has otherwise satisfied his creditors in the meantime so that he is not in debt when he brings suit to recover his property. One who receives title from a person trying to hide his property from his creditors can hold title against his grantor, even though he cannot hold against his grantor's creditors. If he sells the property and keeps the consideration, his grantor cannot have the court's aid to recover what he received for it. The purchaser can hold the property against the true debtor-owner, even though he knew it was conveyed by the debtor to hide it from his creditors.

There is a maxim in law often quoted by the courts and attorneys in such cases; "Whoever comes into a court of equity must come with clean hands."

Loss of Title by Loan

If one lends another person any personal property (the law calls this class of property a chattel) and the use of the property or the possession of it continues for two years without any demand for its return by the lender, the lender has no remedy against the borrower's creditors or purchasers of the property. After that length of time without any demand for return of the property, the ownership is presumed to be with the borrower or one claiming under him in possession of the property.

The lender, however, may still have a right of action against the borrower for conversion (taking property without paying any consideration for it) of the property. He would have a good cause of action if he brings suit within two years after he discovers that the borrower has converted the property, or permitted it to be converted. The lender, in order to protect himself against loss of the loaned property, could have required the borrower to return it before the end of two years, or he could have, at the time of lending, required the borrower to execute a chattel mortgage which the owner could have placed in record in the county where the property was situated, and this would have served as notice of the owner's rights to the property.

A Purchaser of Merchandise at Retail is Protected

One who purchases merchandise from retail dealers is under no obligation to investigate the retailer's authority to sell the merchandise because the law provides that any mortgage, deed of trust, or other form of lien attempted to be given in such an instance shall be void against one who purchases in parcels in the due course of retail business. This statute is a protection for the public.

Deceptive Trade Practices and Consumer Protection

In recent years, consumer protection laws have been passed in many jurisdictions, including Texas. The original Texas Deceptive Trade Practices–Consumer Protection Act was enacted in 1973. It was substantially revised and expanded in 1976. The remedies provided for in the act are not exclusive, but are in addition to any other applicable procedure or remedies of the law. Any purported waiver by a consumer of the provisions of the act is void and unenforceable.

Purpose of the Provisions

The law is designed to protect consumers against false, misleading and deceptive business practices, unconscionable actions, and breaches of warranty. It attempts to provide efficient, economical procedures to enforce these protections.

Deceptive Trade Practices

Deceptive trade practices are declared unlawful and are set out in the act. Article 17.46 (b) lists an extensive number of specific violations, such as passing off goods or services as those of another; representing that goods or services have sponsorship, approval, characteristics, uses, benefits, or qualities they do not have; representing that goods are new if they are secondhand; representing that goods are of a particular standard or quality, if they are of another; advertising goods or services with intent not to sell them as advertised; and resetting the odometer of any motor vehicle so as to reduce the number of miles indicated on the gauge. Other violations are listed.

The statute then provides that a consumer can sue for any of the following:

1. The use or employment by any person of a false, misleading, or deceptive act or practice specifically enumerated in Article 17.46 (b);
2. Breach of an express or implied warranty;
3. Any unconscionable action or course of action by any person; or

4. The employment of any act or practice in violation of the Texas Insurance Code or rules or regulations issued by the state board of insurance.

Damages Available

In a lawsuit, a consumer is entitled to actual damages plus two times that portion of the actual damages that does not exceed $1,000. If the court finds that the conduct of the defendant was committed knowingly, it may award three times the amount of actual damages in excess of $1,000. The court may issue further orders as it deems necessary to protect the consumer.

If, however, there is a finding that the consumer brought the lawsuit in bad faith, or for the purpose of harassment, the court must order the plaintiff (consumer) to pay the defendant's attorney's fees and court costs.

Requirement of Notice and Tender of Settlement

As a prerequisite to filing suit, a consumer must give at least 30 days' written notice to the person to be sued, advising of the specific complaint and the amount of actual damages and expenses, including attorney's fees. A person receiving such a notice may, within 30 days after receipt, tender to the consumer a written offer of settlement. If the consumer rejects the settlement offer, the defendant may file it with the court, and if the court finds that the amount tendered is substantially the same as the actual damages found by the trier of fact, the consumer cannot recover an amount in excess of the amount tendered in the settlement offer or the amount of actual damages found by the trier of fact, whichever is less. The tender of settlement is not an admission of engaging in an unlawful practice.

There are many other provisions of this complex statute; a person facing this kind of problem should consult an attorney with some expertise in this area of law. This law has been the subject of much litigation in recent years.

Corporations, Partnerships, and Limited Partnerships

Corporations

Corporations may be organized under the Texas laws to do business in this state for profit, or they may be organized as non-profit corporations.

The nonprofit corporations often are organized for such under-takings as the dissemination of some religious belief, knowledge of art, promotion of patriotism, or other things not forbidden by law and which are not intended to result in a monetary profit.

Most corporations doing business in this state are for profit. If a corporation obtains its charter from the State of Texas, it is known as a domestic corporation, and if it obtains its charter from some other state, it is known as a foreign corporation. A foreign corporation desiring to do business in the State of Texas must obtain a permit from the secretary of state before starting business within this state. Otherwise, the corporation will be faced with penalties for failure to do so, and it will be at great disadvantage in court if it chooses to sue or is sued in this state.

Two of the principal advantages of doing business as a corpo-ration are: (a) it shields the stockholder from personal liability for causes of action in court against the business, and (b) it affords accumulation of a greater capital aggregate for the business through investments by many persons.

One or more persons may decide to organize a corporation to do business in Texas, and then make application to the secretary of state for a charter. The application must track the statutes and meet all of the requirements and contain all information required by law. Of course, it is necessary to have an attorney to prepare the application since the average person would not know the steps to take. The procedure is not complicated for the one who knows how and is experienced in such matters.

With a proper application and all of the requirements, the secretary of state will issue a "charter" which will show, among other things, the corporation's name, the purpose or purposes for which it is organized, the amount of the authorized capital, and the names and addresses of the incorporators. The charter is the evidence of authority of the corporation to do business in Texas.

To begin business in the state, those interested in the corporation (the stockholders) hold an organizational meeting at which the following things are usually done: (a) a board of directors is elected; (b) by-laws of the corporation are adopted that prescribe the manner in which the corporation is to conduct its business, fill vacancies on the board, etc.; and (c) a corporate seal and form of stock certificate are adopted.

The board of directors then carries on the corporation's business until their successors are elected. To accomplish this, the board of directors elects the corporation's officers, usually a president, a vice president, a secretary, and a treasurer. Large corporations may have any number of other officers which the board may think are necessary to carry on the corporation's business. One person may hold two or more offices in the corporation, but the president of the corporation cannot also be the secretary. Board members may be, and generally are, officers of the corporation.

One who invests money in a corporation receives a stock certificate showing the number of shares he holds in the corporation and usually is entitled to vote at stockholders' meetings, casting his votes according to the number of shares of stock he holds. He also receives income from the corporation according to the number of shares he holds, if the corporation makes profits and pays dividends.

Limited Liability Companies

A new form of business structure is now available in Texas. It is called a limited liability company. It is neither a corporation nor a partnership, although it has attributes of both. Its "articles of organization" must be filed with the Texas Secretary of State. It can be formed by any natural person who is 18 years of age or older. Like a corporation, the owners are protected from personal liability incurred in the operation of the business. Like a corporation, it is also regarded as a separate entity. It must maintain a registered office and a registered agent. It can hold real property in its own name. Yet it has several advantages of a partnership. This form of business may be more widely used as lawyers and businesspeople become more familiar with it.

Partnerships

When two or more persons join together in a business undertaking, sharing profits and losses of the business but without incorporating or filing a declaration in the county clerk's office in the county in which they do business, they are partners. As partners they are collectively, or all of them individually, liable for the debts and other obligations of the business, and one of the partners acting for the partnership will bind the other or all of them.

Many people in business are partners without knowing that they actually occupy such status and that they are individually liable for the whole debt or obligation of the business. For this reason, a wealthy person generally shuns a partnership. He realizes that if the business should become heavily indebted and is required more than all of the business' assets to discharge, he might be sued individually for the deficit.

This is quite different from the status of a stockholder in a corporation. When the corporation's assets have been consumed by creditors, proceedings cannot be brought against the individual stockholders. The stockholder can lose his investment, but with that loss his liability stops—not so with a partnership.

On the other hand, a partnership is a most convenient way for two or more persons to group themselves together to carry on a business. It is not legally necessary that any partnership agreement be put in writing. Two or more persons may agree to start operating a business together and begin work, and they have a partnership—this is known as a general partnership. It is not necessary that their interests in the business be equal. They may be equal, and if there is no agreement between them that one shall have a greater interest, then it is presumed their interests are equal. The partners may agree between the two of them, however, or among the several of them, that one or more of the partners will have a larger interest, and this generally arises when one or more of the partners is equipped to render more service to the business. This is frequently the case when an older doctor or older lawyer takes a young member into the firm.

While it is not legally necessary to the existence of a partnership that a written agreement be signed by the members, it is quite often desirable, and it very frequently is done. The written agreement, which almost always should be prepared by an attorney, lets the partners better understand their relationship, and they are less likely to have misunderstandings in the course of business. There are exceptions to the rule, but when the partnership agreement is drafted by a competent attorney and it is fully understood and signed by the partners, the business is off to a better start, and it is more likely to be successful and to last longer.

The Texas Revised Partnership Act (TRPA) went into effect January 1, 1994. It is a complete revision of the Texas Uniform Partnership Act (TUPA). It applies only to partnerships formed after December 31, 1993, unless an existing partnership elects to be governed by the TRPA. If an existing partnership so elects, it must give notice of this election to third parties with whom it regularly does business. Failure to give notice will nullify the effect of the election as to that party. This statute has created more options for businesses than what existed under the older law. After December 31, 1998, this law applied to all partnerships.

Registered Limited Liability Partnerships

A new form of partnership known as the registered limited liability partnership became authorized in Texas as of January 1, 1994. As with a corporation, specific statutes must be complied with to create this form of partnership. In this structure, it is now possible for a limited partner who is not an active participant in the business to avoid individual liability for debts of the partnership arising from the errors, omissions, incompetence, or malfeasance of other partners. It provides more opportunities for investors and small businesses.

The Limited Partnership

The limited partnership, if it is properly organized and kept on this basis, does afford a limited liability to the "limited partner." In this case, the person of some wealth may be limited in his liability to the amount of money or other things of value he puts into the business. For example, A, who is wealthy, decides to join B and C in a business undertaking. B and C are young and vigorous and they propose to do the work and worry of the business, but they are lacking in capital. A is willing to invest the necessary money for the business to get started, but he feels that he must be protected against personal liability beyond the investment he puts into the business. In other words, he is willing to risk the investment, but he must be protected against suit for more.

So, the three go to their lawyer and have him draft the articles or declaration of the limited partnership, giving the amount each partner is investing in the business and declaring each partner's status. A is a "limited partner" and B and C are "general partners" (the number may be only one or more, and there can be more than one limited partner). With this document properly drawn and executed and filed in each county in which the limited partnership is to do business, A will occupy somewhat the same status as a stockholder in a corporation, but B and C are individually liable for the obligations of the partnership.

Limited partnerships in Texas have also been affected by this law. The statute goes into much more detail about the liability and obligations of general and limited partners. These laws can be found in Volume 17 of *Vernon's Revised Civil Statutes of Texas*.

4. Damage Suits and Complaints

With just daily living, it is not unusual for a person to damage another person or his property. He may negligently bump into another's automobile and damage or destroy it or injure the person. He may dam up a creek on his own land and back water up onto the land of his neighbor upstream and cause damage to growing crops or pasture grasses, or he may spray his own lands to kill weeds and permit the spray to be blown across over his neighbor's land where it kills growing crops or fruit trees. A person may become angry and assault some other person and injure him without good cause, or he may in anger kill some person without good cause. These are a few of the ways he could commit some act that would result in a damage suit. In law, these actions are called torts.

If the person injured or damaged demands retribution and it is not promptly made, the one committing the injury to the person or damage to his property will probably find himself in court answering a damage suit. Sometimes these suits result in judgments for large sums of money. In every instance, however, the damage must be real and not just imagined. For example, when someone is spraying his lands to poison weeds or bushes, the neighbor has no cause for action unless he is actually damaged. It is not sufficient in court that he presents a claim that could result if the spray is blown over his land. It is the duty of the one spraying to exercise care so that he does not permit the spray to be blown over the neighbor's land, and if he uses the spray and the neighbor is not damaged, the neighbor has no cause for action.

There was a case where a land salesman sold a tract of valley land to an unsuspecting purchaser on the premise that the land was in an irrigation district and that irrigation water was available. When the purchaser made preparations to plant crops on the land, he discovered that no irrigation water was available to the land as the seller had assured him. The purchaser went to his lawyer to hire him to bring suit against the seller for actionable fraud. The lawyer asked, "How do you know that the water will not be available at the time you need to irrigate? You have not planted any crops yet, and thus far you have not been damaged. If you go ahead and plant the crops, and then the water is not available, you will then have a cause for damage, since the crops will die and you will thereby suffer a loss."

A person may be damaged by falsely spoken or written words against his character. If someone states publicly, or publishes in a newspaper, etc., or broadcasts over radio or television falsely that a person is dishonest and unworthy of trust, he exposes himself to the possibility that he will be sued for damages by the offended person. If he is unable to sustain the truth of his statements, the damages assessed against him may be very great. A judgment may be rendered against him for actual or compensatory damages and, in addition, punitive or exemplary damage to punish him for a great wrong.

If the person libeled was a public figure, however, the burden of proof on the plaintiff is heavier. He or she must prove not only that the statement was false and injurious, but also that it was done with malice. Malice means the defendant either knew the statement was false or was intentionally reckless as to its truth.

It is not only public officials, along with priests, ministers, and rabbis, who are entitled to collect damages; any other persons can have the aid of the courts in claiming damages for wrongs against them. It is interesting, though, that a remark made and published about one person may give rise to a damage suit, whereas if it is made about another, it can have no damaging effect. An example is where a statement published about a businessman indicating he is insolvent and cannot pay his bills may be greatly damaging to him and give rise to a damage suit, but if the same remark is made about a member of the clergy it may not be damaging at all; in fact it may be beneficial to him if his parishioners become aware of the situation.

The Cause of Action

Lawsuits for damages may be filed in a variety of situations based upon various legal theories.

Intentional Injury

If A hits B in the mouth, knocking out several teeth, not only can B file criminal charges against A, he can also file a civil law-suit demanding that A pay for the damage to his teeth, his medical bills, and money for pain and suffering. In addition, where there was intentional injury, the judge or jury can award punitive damages to B. This is not to compensate B for his losses, but simply to punish A. It can be a windfall to B, especially if A's actions are so extreme as to anger the jury and cause them to return a large amount of punitive damages.

Several years ago, in a Texas medical malpractice case against a hospital involving the death of a young mother who had just given birth, the jury awarded actual damages of two million dollars. The jury's anger against the hospital's actions, however, was expressed by their award of punitive damages in the amount of five million dollars.

Negligence

Simple negligence is the basis on which most civil lawsuits are filed. To establish a case of negligence, the plaintiff must demonstrate three things before he is entitled to recover damages.

First, he must show that the defendant has a duty toward him. It may be a duty based on contract, or it may be simply the duty of a citizen to conduct himself in a safe and reasonable manner and in compliance with law. But without a duty, there is no basis for a lawsuit. For example, suppose Henry is standing on the end of a pier and sees Sam drowning in water about eight feet from the pier. There is a ten-foot pole on the pier, which could easily be used to rescue Sam. Henry, however, just stands there and watches Sam drown. If Henry and Sam are strangers (and Henry is not the lifeguard), Sam's family has no lawsuit against Henry. Henry had no legal duty to come to the aid of a stranger.

Second, the plaintiff must show that the defendant deviated from or failed to measure up to that duty. This is put to the jury in terms of what the reasonably prudent person would have done in the same circumstances.

Finally, the plaintiff must show that the defendant's actions were the cause of the plaintiff's damages.

Strict Liability

In recent years, strict liability (also known as products liability) has become an extremely important area of law. It is a modern development, a response to the complexities of an industrialized society. It imposes liability, without regard to fault or negligence, upon the seller or manufacturer of a product that is dangerous to the consumer, if in fact the consumer is injured.

The doctrine is applicable only if the seller is in the business of selling the product, and the product reaches the consumer without substantial change in the condition in which it is sold. The law is based on public policy. It developed as the courts decided that the costs of injuries resulting from defective products should be borne, as a cost of doing business, by the persons who put the products into the channels of commerce, rather than by the injured parties, who usually have no power to protect themselves.

The doctrine has been applied to all kinds of products, from bottles and containers to toys. It has been the basis of numerous suits against automobile manufacturers.

Suppose a person buys a new auto. Two days after the purchase, the steering wheel on the auto locks while he or she is driving on a Dallas freeway. The person survives the resulting crash, but suffers severe injuries. Under the doctrine of strict liability, he or she does not have to prove that the manufacturer or dealership was negligent. All the victim needs to show is where the car was purchased and that the steering had not been tampered with or worked on following the purchase. The car owner is then entitled to damages.

A new application of the doctrine in Texas was recently made to a hospital that had furnished a patient with a paper gown. The patient lit a cigarette, and the gown caught fire, inflicting injuries from which the patient eventually died. The hospital was held liable under principles of strict liability.

Limitation of Personal Actions

As in suits for regaining possession of land, there are also limitations of time in which one may bring suits in personal actions. If the one having the right to sue permits the limitation period to pass without bringing his suit, he loses his right to sue.

Actions to be Commenced in One Year

1. Actions for malicious prosecution or for injuries done to the character or reputation of another by libel or slander.

2. Actions for damages for seduction, or breach of promise of marriage.

In these instances, death of the injured person or death of the one doing the wrong will not extinguish the right to bring the suit if it is brought within the time period. Suit can be brought on behalf of the injured person in the name of his estate, if the injured one has died, and against the estate of the one committing the wrong, if that one has died.

Actions to be Commenced in Two Years

1. Actions of trespass for injury done to the estate or property of another.
2. Actions for detaining the personal property of another, and for converting the property to one's own use.
3. Actions for taking and carrying away the goods and chattels of another.
4. Actions for injury done to another person.
5. Actions of forcible entry and forcible detainer.
6. Actions against a city government or the commissioners' court, and others that may be involved, for the closing of a street or roadway and relinquishing possession of the land that the street or roadway occupied. Then anyone not in possession of the land but claiming it or an interest in it, or claiming that the street or roadway should be reopened, must bring his suit within the two-year period or lose his right to sue on the cause. The one in possession of the land abandoned for street or roadway purposes will gain full title to the land by possessing it for two years, if during the two-year period he is undisturbed by any suit to recover it.

Actions to be Commenced in Three Years

All actions for or against carriers involving controversies over freight charges must be filed within three years after the cause of action accrues.

Actions to be Commenced in Four Years

In the following cases, suit must be filed within four years after the cause of action has accrued, and not afterward:

1. Actions for debt.
2. Actions for the penalty or for damages on the penal clause of a bond to convey real estate.
3. Actions by one partner against his co-partner for a settlement of the partnership accounts, actions upon stated or open accounts, or upon mutual and current accounts concerning the trade of merchandise between merchant and merchant, their factors or agents. The cause of action shall be considered as having accrued on a cessation of the dealings in which they were interested together.
4. Suits for recovery on the bond of any executor, administrator, or guardian. The four-year period commences upon the death, resignation, removal, or discharge of the executor, administrator, or guardian.
5. Actions on foreign judgments—where judgment has been rendered in some other state, in the District of Columbia, or in some foreign country—will be barred in this state, if such action is also barred in the place where the judgment was rendered.
6. Actions requiring the specific performance of a contract for the conveyance of land.
7. Actions involving the contest of any will. The four-year period runs from the date that the will is admitted to probate. If

the action is based upon a claim of forgery or fraud in the making of the will, the action may be brought within four years after the discovery of the forgery or fraud.

8. All other actions, other than for recovery of land, where the law has not provided a specific limitation period shall be barred in four years.

Actions to be Commenced in Ten Years

A lawsuit against an architect, engineer, or builder, for negligence in the construction or repair of an improvement or equipment attached to real property, must be brought within 10 years after completion. This will be extended an additional two years from the date of claim, if a claim for indemnity is filed within the ten-year period.

An action against a person who has resided in this state for 10 years prior to the action may not be brought on a foreign judgment rendered more than 10 years before the commencement of the action in this state.

Tolling the Statute of Limitation

In certain situations, time is not counted under a statute of limitations. The statute does not "run" against a person younger than 18, or a person of unsound mind. The time does not begin to be counted until the disability is removed. If, for example, an act of medical malpractice is committed against a five-year-old child, the two-year statute does not begin to be counted (i.e., does not "run") until the child reaches 18. She would have until age 20 to file suit.

Limitation After Death

In case of the death of a person against whom or in whose favor there may be a cause of action, the law of limitation is suspended until 12 months after his death, unless an executor or administrator qualifies prior to that time. In that event, the running of limitation is delayed only until such qualification.

If the full limitation period has run against the right to sue, no acknowledgment of the justness of the claim made subsequent to the time it became due can be admitted as evidence at the trial, unless the acknowledgment is in writing and is signed by the person to be charged.

In making contracts, persons, firms, or corporations cannot legally agree or stipulate to shorten the time for suing to less than two years.

No limitation is effective against the state, a county, a city, or a school district, meaning any of these organizations can bring suit against one in possession of its land in disregard of the limitation periods already discussed. However long a "squatter" may stay in possession of land belonging to one of these organizations, he cannot perfect his title to it.

Abatement of Nuisances

Incorporated cities generally have power and authority under their charters to abate nuisances, which is the stopping or preventing of a nuisance. This is particularly true where the health of citizens of the city is endangered, some sanitation ordinance is being violated so that disease is likely to spread, or where some constantly annoying noise is maintained to disturb the rest of people and endanger health. An example is a family who keeps livestock such as cows, hogs, or chickens penned in the backyard in violation of a city ordinance, thus attracting flies or rats to the neighborhood; or the animals make loud and disturbing noises at night, disturbing sleep. Another situation is where a nearby neighbor keeps dogs penned close to another person's house and fails to keep the pen sanitary, and it creates a health hazard; or the dogs howl and bark at night and disturb the neighborhood residents' sleep.

The city will generally aid a complainant in instances of this kind and bring action against the offending party and abate the nuisance. It is fairly easy to obtain relief if the complainant can show that the acts in question constitute a violation of a city ordinance. It is more difficult if the one creating the nuisance is carrying on a business not forbidden by ordinance. In such an instance the city may not be willing to give its aid, and the complainant may have to bring suit and try to prove the validity of his complaint.

By law, the following acts are declared to be common nuisances: knowingly maintaining a place to which persons habitually go for prostitution, illegal gambling, or the delivery of illegal controlled substances. An individual or the state, acting through the attorney general or local prosecutors, can sue to stop this activity. The winning party is awarded reasonable attorney's fees and court costs. This makes it more realistic for individuals to sue in situations where state and local authorities are unwilling or unable to act.

Another statute defines a public nuisance as follows:

1. Gambling, gambling promotion, or communicating gambling information prohibited by law;
2. Promotion or aggravated promotion of prostitution;
3. Compelling prostitution;
4. Commercial manufacture, commercial distribution, or commercial exhibition of obscene material;
5. Commercial exhibition of live dances or other acts depicting real or simulated sexual intercourse or deviate sexual intercourse;
6. Engaging in a voluntary fight between a man and a bull if there is wagering or an admission fee is charged; or

7. Delivering or using a controlled substance in violation of the Texas Controlled Substances Act.

As with the common nuisance, suit can be brought by state prosecutors or individuals. These remedies are often used against adult bookstores, massage parlors, and, more recently, crack houses that are located in residential areas.

When a place is kept for gambling, or is a disorderly or bawdy house, any interested citizen may bring suit to abate the nuisance. If proper proof is given, an injunction to prevent the continued use of the place for such purposes can be obtained. While a private citizen can bring and prosecute such a suit, it is better to seek the aid of law enforcement officers first.

There are other nuisances that are borderline, such as the blowing of automobile horns disturbingly near one's home, bad odors from manufacturing plants, or the spilling of garbage on the street in front of one's home. These nuisances are often too difficult to abate, maybe because the acts are not consistently repeated, or the offender cannot be definitely identified. Anyone intending personally to abate a nuisance would do well to explain his complaint to an attorney and receive an opinion from him as to whether he has a provable case, before he incurs other expense. But this does not mean that one should hesitate to abate a continuing, unnecessary annoyance which could be proved to be a real nuisance.

Worker's Compensation Insurance

Prior to the enactment of the Workmen's Compensation Laws, it was brought to the legislature's attention that many workers were being injured, and sometimes killed, in the course of their work. It was pointed out that often there was no kind of compensation available for the injured, or for the relatives of the ones who lost their lives. If a worker was injured on the job, or if he lost his life accidentally, then under the common law rule, he, or those representing him after his death, had to prove that his employer was negligent and that the negligence brought about the injury or death. This proof was the only basis for recovering damages against the employer.

If the proof could not be given, recovery was not made, even though the worker may never be able to work again because of his injury, or his family would be forced into poverty because of his death. In trying such cases, the employer could defeat recovery by showing that the injury or death was caused by acts of a fellow workman; that the injured workman was negligent and caused or contributed to the injury or death; or that the worker knew of the danger involved and assumed the risk of the employment.

Moreover, it often happened that if the injured worker or the representatives of the worker who lost his life did succeed in proving negligence on the employer's part, there still could be no compensation recovered because the employer was financially unable to respond.

These conditions resulted in great hardship for workers, and it posed a threat to employers. An employer was constantly in danger of being brought to financial ruin by a lawsuit from an employee. This sometimes made able individuals, who were fully capable of furnishing extensive employment to people of this state, reluctant to become employers. This reluctance tended to slow down commerce and reduce full employment and lessen opportunities for workmen.

It became apparent that legislation was necessary to establish some kind of plan to protect the worker and his family regardless of the fact that the worker recognized and assumed the risk of the employment; that he was injured through no negligence of the employer; that he, himself, was negligent and that his negligence contributed to his injury; or that his injury resulted from acts of a fellow worker. On the other hand, it was recognized that individuals willing and able to run businesses and furnish employment must be protected against damage suits that could penalize them out of business.

The Worker's Compensation Law (by statute in 1977, the term "Workmen's Compensation" was changed to "Worker's Compensation") was adopted to fill these needs. It requires every employer with one or more employees to carry worker's compensation insurance, except persons, firms, or corporations operating any steam, electric, street, or interurban railway as a common carrier. These exceptions are governed by other laws. The law does not apply to those employing domestic servants or casual employees engaged in employment incidental to a personal residence. If an employer does not subscribe to the insurance and comply with the other requirements of the law, then he operates at his own risk.

If an employee is injured while working, the employer cannot defend himself in court on the grounds that: (a) the employee assumed the risk of the work involved; (b) the injury or death of the employee was caused by acts of a fellow worker; or (c) the injury or death was caused in whole or in part by negligence of the employee himself. These are the three defenses once used by employers to defeat most employee lawsuits. In addition, if the employee wins, there is no limit to the amount of damages he can recover.

This is a real whip to make employers comply with the law. If an employer complies with the law, then he is not subject to damage suits by his employees for their injuries or deaths suffered while on the job. The employees must file their claims with the Texas Workers' Compensation Commission in Austin, which administers the law. This commission will hear the employee's case and make an award. If the employee is not satisfied with the award, he can appeal his case to the district court, and from there, to the Court of Appeals.

An employer who is to be protected under the law is required to give notice to his employees by posting notices in the plant or other place where the employees work that he subscribes to the insurance. If he fails to give the notice, he is not protected. The employee will be subject to the law's provisions, unless at the time of his employment he gives his employer notice in writing that he expects to exercise his rights under the common law with respect to injuries or death that he may suffer in the course of his employment. If he gives such a notice, and he is permitted to work after the notice is given, then the employer would not be protected against a damage suit by that employee for injuries he may receive, but the common law defenses would be available to him.

The New Workers' Compensation Act

The 1989 legislature enacted a major revision of the Texas Workers' Compensation Act. Injuries that occurred before January 1, 1991, however, are still covered by the old law. The changes are comprehensive and controversial. One major effect has been to pretty much take out the financial incentive for attorneys to become involved.

Notice of Claims and Payment of Benefits

An injured employee must notify his employer of the injury within 30 days after it occurs. Failure to do this relieves the employer and the insurance company of liability. In addition, the injured employee must file a "claim for compensation" with the Workers' Compensation Commission not later than one year after the injury occurs. The employer must file a written report with the commission if the employee is absent from work for more than one day due to the injury.

Under the new statute, employee benefits are called "income benefits." They are computed differently than under the old statute. The employee is paid a percentage of his average weekly salary, depending on his "impairment rating" as determined using the guidelines published by the American Medical Association.

The employee shall be entitled to a maximum weekly amount not greater than 70 percent of the state average weekly wage. The minimum weekly income must be no less than 15 percent of the state average weekly wage. The Texas Employment Commission must determine these maximum and minimum amounts on September 1 of each year. This amount is calculated by determining the average weekly wage of manufacturing production workers in Texas.

The commission can make hardship advances to workers, once it is determined that income benefits will probably be paid. The employee must apply for this and must be able to demonstrate financial hardship.

The law calls for an ombudsman program to assist workers and their families. These people are to assist unrepresented claimants and other parties to make sure their rights in the Workers' Compensation system are protected. All employers are required by law to notify their employees of the ombudsman program.

The new statute has been moved to Section 401 ff of the Texas Labor Code.

What To Do When Sued

When suit is brought against anyone for any cause, a "citation" will be served upon the person being sued, which is the official notice from the court, signed by the court clerk or his deputy. The citation shows when the suit was filed and by whom, and the nature of the cause of action, and indicates the time in which the person sued should answer in court.

This notice should not be ignored, for if it is, a default judgment will be entered in the case against the person being sued. The law assumes that if the allegations in the plaintiff's petition are not denied, they are true, and a judgment will be rendered on the plaintiff's petition without a trial. The defendant, the one who is sued, should take the citation to his attorney, talk the case over with him, and arrange employment and the amount of the attorney fee to be paid. It does not suffice that the cause stated appears to be unfounded or unjust. If it is indeed an unfounded case, it will be easy to defend if it is handled by a capable lawyer.

However simplified we seek to make court procedure, it is too technical for the layman, and if he does undertake to defend himself without the assistance of a lawyer, he may overlook the most fundamental defense at his command and lose the case on a technicality. The petition itself may be defective so that an advantage could be gained by initially lodging an exception against it, or a plea in abatement, and this defect ordinarily would not be detected by one not skilled in court procedure. The judge might be sympathetic, but he is the judge, and he cannot serve as the advocate for either party in court.

The judge and the jury are bound by the law and the facts proved by admissible evidence in the case, and the defendant must be prepared with his evidence. The strict rules of evidence, which are not in easy reach of any layman and which often are the lawyer's hardest work in a case, may defeat the unskilled. These rules work both ways, and no one dares go into court unprepared to use them in keeping out testimony, exhibits, etc., which do not belong in the case. If any of this material does get in over objections, then proper exceptions should be preserved so that the wrong can be considered on appeal, if an appeal is taken.

Moreover, answering the plaintiff's petition is a technical matter which requires a lawyer. As mentioned, it is sometimes necessary to file and urge preliminary pleas before answering to the merits of the case. Sometimes a case can be won by an exception, or plea in abatement, and by presenting the laws applicable to the allegations in the plaintiff's petition. The average person could hardly be expected to be acquainted with such procedures, much less how to meet the various legal strategies that may be used against him during the trial.

One should rarely, if ever, decide to represent oneself in a lawsuit that amounts to more than a small sum, and even in these small cases he is likely to have fewer regrets if he employs a competent legal counselor. It has been said that, "One who represents himself in court has a fool for a client." There is some virtue in knowing when to be cautious.

Arbitration

Arbitration in its simplest form is a method of settling disputes without going to court. Example: A and B have made an agreement to cultivate a certain tract of land with the understanding that they will contribute equally in labor and expenses and share the returns in the same way, but during the busy season one of them gets sick and is unable to do as much as the other; thus a dispute arises. When the harvest is in and the returns are to be divided, there is a difference of opinion between them as to how much each should receive out of the net returns. When each one concludes that the other is unreasonable, they call in C, who is a disinterested party and known by both of them to be a fair man. They agree that if C will decide between them they will each be bound by his decision. C accepts the responsibility, hears both sides, and makes his award to each, which they accept. They have settled their dispute by arbitration.

This is a very quick, inexpensive and effective way of arriving at a settlement. By this method, the dispute was settled in a day or two or an hour or two when, had the parties gone to court, they may not have had the settlement in weeks, months, or a year or two. The key to the quick settlement here was the agreement by the parties that they would be bound by the arbitrator's decision.

But arbitration does not always carry with it the disputants' agreement that they will be bound by the arbitrator's decision. One might agree to an arbitration of the dispute reserving the right to appeal.

The Uniform Arbitration Act

This area is controlled by the Texas version of the Uniform Arbitration Act. The statute validates an agreement to submit an existing controversy to arbitration. It makes valid an arbitration agreement in an existing contract, should disagreements arise as to the effect or meaning of the contract. The statute does not apply to:

(1) Collective bargaining agreements
(2) A contract for the purchase of real property for less than $50,000 by an individual unless signed by the parties and their attorneys
(3) A claim for personal injury unless approved by the claimant's attorney, or a claim for worker's compensation

The method of appointing arbitrators as detailed in an arbitration agreement should be followed. If the agreement contains no such provision and the parties cannot agree, a court will make the appointment. The arbitrators will appoint a time and place for hearing and notify all parties. The arbitrators have the power to subpoena witnesses, administer oaths, and authorize depositions for witnesses who are unable to attend the hearing.

The award must be in writing and signed by the arbitrators. Within 90 days, either party can file an application to vacate the award in a court having proper jurisdiction. Such an application will be granted only where there was corruption, fraud, or any other irregularity in the arbitration process. If the application to vacate is denied, the court will confirm the award.

Alternative Dispute Resolution

In 1987, the legislature passed a statute that allows a court to refer a pending dispute for an alternative dispute resolution procedure, usually mediation. Referrals can be made to special judges, county dispute resolution systems, or private persons or groups who offer their services to the public. Mediation occurs when a third party informally listens to both sides of a dispute, then confers with both sides to help them reach a settlement of the dispute. Some courts require all parties to go through mediation before their case can go to trial.

Civil Trial Procedure

There are complaints from both lawyers and lay people about the waste of time in the courtroom. Many lawyers feel the least productive use of their time is at the courthouse. There is truth to these complaints. But this is surely the price that must be paid for a system that attempts to find a fair and just resolution to every dispute. Good judges try to save time for everyone concerned if it can be done without losing the court's ultimate goal of justice for the parties. When two Texas citizens, however, or any others who have a right to, come into court for a redress of wrongs or for a defense of rights, the main duties call for the best that democracy can give, and the necessary time required to attain it becomes relatively unimportant.

The judge is bound by the duties of his high office to conduct a fair and impartial trial, and the lawyers are bound by their profession and by law to represent their clients to the best of their abilities. Indeed, the judge and the lawyers are subject to heavy penalties provided by law and professional associations for failure to discharge their duties. The jury is under oath to give a fair and impartial verdict according to the evidence and the law presented to them. The witnesses are sworn to tell the truth and the law provides severe penalties if they fail to do so.

In most cases, trials are well-conducted, court personnel do their duty, and justice is achieved. The American system of jurisprudence, based on the English common-law and defined and delineated by the United States and Texas constitutions and laws, is one of the world's best systems for settling disputes. It has flaws and shortcomings, but stands up well when compared to other systems.

Origin

Trial procedures developed from methods used in settling family disputes, because the family was the earliest organized unit of society. It still remains the basic one. Before there were any courts, families, by necessity, had rules—not written rules, but rules, nevertheless—that were understood. The father was first in command, the mother second, and then the children in order of age.

In any family, disputes arise among children, and a wise parent will take time to listen to the children about both sides of the question. Each child involved should be permitted to tell his side of the story without interruption from the opposition, letting each child name his witnesses to bear out his testimony. The parent's wisdom and the information from the children help make the decisions that set things right.

This is a trial and trial procedure in its simplest form, and it is the natural beginning of respect for law and order. As children grow up, they learn to appreciate the need for justice and lend their efforts toward its effectiveness.

Since disputes arise outside of the family where parental authority does not extend, however, it became necessary to establish some authority with jurisdiction over families and individuals and their relationships with each other. And so, over a considerable time, we have arrived at the present system designed for orderly solutions to disputes. We have gone to great lengths to provide means for settling disputes around the council table. We believe that when people grow in wisdom and moral being, they are willing to use the council table for settling disputes, instead of trial by physical combat.

Suppose a controversy has arisen between two citizens of this state, and it has grown out of complicated and involved business so that each person honestly believes that he is right, or at any rate, each one has decided to go through a lawsuit rather than yield to the other. One person has made his demands upon the other and has served notice that unless his demands are met a suit will be filed to enforce them. His demands are flatly refused.

So, the first person explains the whole matter to a lawyer. The lawyer decides from the story that it is a dispute that can be settled only by litigation, and he becomes the person's representative. He may talk to the opposing party, or write him one or two letters, but he soon draws up a petition to the district court. He then calls his client in and reads the petition to him, and they agree that the cause of action is correctly stated. The person who is starting the suit is called the "plaintiff," and the person against whom the suit is brought is called the "defendant," which is how they are referred to in the petition which the lawyer is preparing to file.

The plaintiff gives his lawyer the filing fee required by the district court clerk, and the lawyer files the petition in the district court. Besides defining the purpose of the suit, this petition requests that the defendant be cited to appear and answer the suit, and that the plaintiff be granted the relief to which he is entitled. The lawyer gives a copy of the petition to the clerk so it can be delivered to the defendant when he is served the citation which the clerk will issue.

The district court clerk will immediately issue a citation, which is the official notice from the court to the defendant that he is being sued, what the suit is about, stating the date on which the defendant must answer.

The clerk sends the citation, with a copy of the plaintiff's petition attached, to the county sheriff, or his deputy, or to a constable, and the citation instructs the officer to serve it upon the defendant. The officer serves the citation with the attached petition upon the defendant. Thus, the defendant knows that he has been sued, the amount or other relief asked by the plaintiff, and the date on or before which he must file his answer.

Now the defendant usually hires a lawyer to defend him in the case. The defendant's lawyer prepares and files his answer in the case within the limited time. In that answer, the defendant's lawyer denies everything, not admitting anything stated in the plaintiff's petition, thereby putting all the plaintiff's claims in issue. He or she then sends a copy to the plaintiff's lawyer.

So each side is then aware of the nature of the pending fight. Both sides talk to prospective witnesses, each trying to find those whose testimony can help its own purpose or defeat the opposition.

At this point the process of "discovery" begins. This is the method by which each party can find out about the evidence in possession of the other side. It involves written interrogatories, requests for admissions, oral depositions and motions to produce.

The process was intended to end the old practice of "trial by surprise" and encourage settlements by giving both parties full access to the facts of the case. In reality, it became a means by which the parties could harass each other and sometimes bring poorly financed parties to defeat. Because of these abuses, the Texas Supreme Court in 1998 issued new rules restricting the use of discovery procedures. Discovery nevertheless continues to be a critical and often expensive part of a civil case.

Before the trial date, the attorneys will make sure that witnesses are summoned to attend the trial, unless they are satisfied that the witnesses will attend without a summons. Also, before the trial date, one side or the other decides that the trial should be before a jury. That side then deposits a jury fee with the district clerk and requests a jury for the trial.

On the trial date, the court calls for order and the clerk reads the case's number and style, and the judge asks the attorneys if they are ready for trial. If one or the other is not ready, the judge will hear his excuse and grant a delay, or he will overrule the motion for delay or postponement. If both sides announce ready, the clerk will order the jury panel to stand and hold up their right hands and be sworn in.

The clerk will then hand the plaintiff's attorney and the defendant's attorney identical lists containing 24 names. The attorney for the plaintiff will tell the jury panel the nature of the lawsuit and then question the panel as a group about their qualifications. If he finds any he believes to be disqualified to serve on the jury, he will address the judge and "challenge the juror for cause." The judge will rule on the challenge and sustain or overrule it. If he sustains it, the person's name is erased from the list. If he overrules it the name is left on the list, which means that the judge does not believe that the person is disqualified.

After this general questioning, the plaintiff's attorney may question members of the panel individually, to learn more about their individual attitudes toward the kind of case that is to be tried and other pertinent facts. This is called *voir dire*.

Next, the defendant's attorney will make his statement about the nature of the case to be tried, and he will question the panel in much the same manner as the plaintiff's attorney did, but, of course, seeking to eliminate those who may be disqualified or who may have some prejudice that would be against the interests of the defendant. If the challenges made for cause by the attorneys and sustained by the judge reduce the number on the panel to less than 24, the judge will call for additional prospective jurors to bring the number on the lists back to 24, and the new ones called are questioned by the attorneys.

With the challenges for cause disposed of and the number on the lists brought back to 24, each side is allowed six "peremptory challenges" or "scratches," which are made by simply drawing a line through the names of the objectionable ones without the necessity of stating a reason. Attorneys may not, however, scratch jurors because of their race. Thus a full panel of 12 jurors are left on the list after each side makes six scratches, even if each side scratches different names.

After the attorneys have made their scratches and have handed the clerk their changed lists, the clerk reads out the first 12 unscratched names, and these file into the jury box as their names are called. After they are in place, the judge, or the clerk under the judge's direction, will command the jurors to stand, raise their right hands, and be sworn in with the following oath: "You, and each of you, do solemnly swear that in all cases between parties which shall be to you submitted, you will a true verdict render, according to the law as it may be given you in charge by the court and to the evidence submitted to you under the rulings of the court, so help you God."

If the witnesses have not been sworn in previously, the clerk will order all witnesses in the case to stand and raise their right hands and be sworn in with the following oath: "You and each of you do solemnly swear that the evidence which you are about to give in this case will be the truth, the whole truth, and nothing but the truth, so help you God."

It may be desirable to the attorney on either side, or both of them, to have witnesses "put under the rule." Either attorney may address the court, "Your Honor, we invoke the rule." Whereupon the judge will tell the witnesses that the rule has been invoked and that they should remain outside the courtroom until their names are called to testify and that they should not discuss the case among themselves or with anyone else. The witnesses then leave the courtroom, but remain in the halls where they can hear their names as they are called to the witness chair. The judge will order the attorneys to proceed.

The attorneys for each side are then entitled to make opening statements, telling the jury the nature of their claim and the facts they expect to prove. The party with the burden of proof for the entire case (usually the plaintiff) has the right to speak first. From this point on, a court reporter will take down almost everything that is said in open court.

After this, the plaintiff's attorney will introduce his evidence by calling to the witness chair one witness at a time and asking questions designed to draw testimony that will establish the plaintiff's claim.

The defendant's attorney will cross-examine, if he chooses, each witness as he concludes his direct testimony.

As the questioning by the plaintiff's attorney proceeds, exhibits are offered in evidence. The defendant's attorney will object to any question which he believes calls for inadmissible testimony, or to evidence and exhibits that he thinks are not proper for the plaintiff to offer (in fact, to any testimony and exhibits that he hopes to keep out). He gives his reasons for the objection such as, "It is hearsay," or, "The question is leading" (meaning that the attorney suggests the answer he expects by the way he asks his question), or, "It is irrelevant and immaterial to any issue in this case," or other reasons why he thinks the testimony should not be admitted.

As he makes his objections, counsel stands and addresses the judge thusly: "Your Honor, we object to the question because it is irrelevant and immaterial."

The judge will immediately rule on the objection by "sustaining" the objection, which means that the witness should not answer the question, or by "overruling" the objection, which means that the witness should answer the question.

Sometimes the attorneys' views differ so greatly on what should be admitted and what should not be admitted in evidence that arguments develop over points of law. Often, in a closely contested proceeding, the judge will have the jury leave the courtroom while the judge hears argument from the attorneys and then rules on the dispute. This part of the proceeding is also recorded by the stenographer, for it will compose part of the case's record. The attorneys, for both sides, must assure that the record is well-made so that if he is ruled against wrongly by the judge, the error may be righted on appeal, if an appeal is taken.

The plaintiff's attorney must continue with the introduction of evidence until he has "made out his case," for if he does not prove a bona fide cause of action, he will, upon proper motion of the defendant's attorney, lose his case. The judge will instruct the jury to find for the defendant, which is known as an "instructed verdict." But an attorney with a well-prepared case will not stop short. He will develop his case fully and to the point where, in the absence of contrary proof by the defendant, he will win his case. If he has made out a bona fide case, and the defendant can offer nothing to disprove it, then an "instructed verdict" will result for the plaintiff.

Finally, the plaintiff's attorney exhausts his supply of evidence, and he concludes that he should "rest" his case.

When the plaintiff's attorney rests, the defendant's attorney will probably make a motion for an instructed verdict for the defendant, claiming that the plaintiff has not presented a bona fide case. The judge will rule on the motion by granting it or overruling it. If he grants the motion, the case comes to an abrupt end in the defendant's favor, which does not happen often. If he overrules the motion, the burden of proceeding shifts to the defendant. This means that the judge believes the plaintiff has stated and proven a bona fide case and if the defendant does not properly refute it, the plaintiff should have a judgment against the defendant.

This is somewhat like ball players shifting from "field" to "bat." The defendant must be heard if he desires to be heard, and he almost always does.

The defendant's attorney will then state briefly the nature of his defense and the facts relied on to support it. The defendant's attorney will then introduce his evidence in an effort to disprove or tear down the case that has just been made out against his client. As he puts his witnesses on the stand and questions them in an effort to elicit testimony favorable to the defendant, the opposing attorney objects to questions which he thinks call for inadmissible testimony; and he has a right to cross examine each witness at the conclusion of the direct testimony.

The defendant's attorney proceeds with witness after witness, and with exhibits, to show his side of the lawsuit favorably until he has covered as best he can the whole scope of defense, because both the defendant and the plaintiff will be confined, after the defendant rests, to rebutting the testimony or evidence.

After all of the defendant's evidence has been presented, the plaintiff may introduce further testimony to rebut that given by the defendant, but he cannot offer any new testimony as original evidence, except in particular instances when the judge believes it is necessary to arrive at justice.

After all the rebuttal evidence offered by the plaintiff is in, the defendant may offer testimony to rebut that last offered by the plaintiff.

After all of the evidence on both sides is in, the judge will prepare his charge to the jury with the assistance of the attorneys on both sides. Each side is given a copy of the charge before it is given to the jury, and time is allowed for the attorneys to prepare written objections, which they file with the court reporter, as the charge itself is filed, as part of the case's record.

Finally, when the issues are composed and the judge is satisfied with them, and the exceptions by the attorneys have been recorded, the judge will read the charge to the jury, and he will also read the definitions he considers necessary and give explanatory instructions, but he will not comment on the evidence or the credibility of the witnesses.

Following the charge to the jury by the judge, the attorneys are permitted to address the jury, first the plaintiff's attorney and then the defendant's attorney, followed by a rebuttal by the plaintiff's attorney. The judge will allow them the time he believes the nature of the case demands.

After the attorneys' arguments are concluded, the jury retires to consider its verdict. If they agree, they return into open court with their verdict in writing, and the foreman of the jury hands the written verdict to the clerk. The judge calls the court to order and inquires whether they have reached a verdict. If they answer that they have, the judge directs the clerk to read it.

The clerk reads the jury's verdict. The losing party generally requests a poll of the jury and this request is always granted. To poll the jury, the verdict is read to them collectively, whether it be on a general charge or on special issues, then they are asked individually if that is their verdict. If any juror answers negatively, the jury is sent back for further deliberation. Either side has the right to require a poll of the jury.

Once the jury has agreed and has returned its verdict, the judge renders the judgment in the case based upon that verdict.

As a practical matter, the winning party's attorney prepares and submits to the judge a draft of the judgment he thinks should be rendered in the case, also giving a copy to the opposing counsel for his consideration. The opposing counsel may offer suggestions for some change, or he may even write and submit to the judge and the opposing counsel the kind of judgment he thinks should be entered in the case. Ultimately, the judge approves and enters one of these drafts or makes changes and then approves and enters it as the judgment, or he may write it entirely by himself and enter it as the judgment in the case.

The foregoing is the basic procedure in a trial before a jury. In civil cases like this example, the trial also can be held before the judge without a jury. In fact, if no jury is requested in advance, the trial is before the judge only.

The procedure is the same, except for the absence of the jury, but it is also somewhat more informal before the judge.

Number of Jurors

For many years, a jury verdict had to be unanimous, and the loss of a jury member meant a mistrial. This has changed. Today it is sufficient if any 10 of the 12 members agree on all issues. In addition, as many as three of the jurors can die or become disabled, and the remaining nine can render a verdict.

New Trial

Often the losing party will make a motion for a new trial. In this motion he states the errors which he thinks have been made in the case which entitle him to a new trial. When this motion is made, the judge generally will grant a hearing on it, at which the attorneys on each side will present to the judge their views of the law and its application to the procedure in the case.

The winner tries to avoid a new trial and the loser tries to obtain one. The judge will grant or overrule the motion. If the motion is granted, then a new trial is ordered, unless the loser on the motion appeals from the judge's ruling.

In some instances, the case will go up to a higher court on the judge's ruling on the motion, and the question is ruled on by the Court of Appeals. If the judge overrules the motion for a new trial, the mover (the losing party), if he believes he is right and the amount involved is worth the effort and expense, gives notice of appeal.

Appeal

When notice of appeal is made within the prescribed time, then the one taking the appeal, in order to get to the higher court, must post an appeal bond in an amount determined by the judge, or the clerk, to cover adequately the costs (in the court below and the estimated costs in the court above) for the reason that additional costs will be incurred on appeal. The bond may be in cash and posted with the clerk, or it may be by an approved bonding company or by two or more persons who have sufficient assets.

After an adequate bond is posted with the clerk, the appellant may then order a transcript of the record in the case and take or send it to the Court of Appeals. The appeal is almost wholly a function of the attorneys in the case, since no new testimony can be presented to the appellate court, and no witnesses can testify before that court. The case goes before the appellate court on the record made in the court below and the briefs that are presented by the attorneys in the case and their oral argument at the hearing.

The Court of Appeals may affirm the initial judgment or reverse it. If that court affirms the initial judgment without change, then it is up to the appellant to take the case on to the Supreme Court of Texas, if it is a controversy that qualifies for consideration by that highest court; otherwise, he has lost the case, and the initial judgment will be enforced.

The Court of Appeals may reverse the initial judgment and remand the case for a new trial (which means that the motion for a new trial in the court below should have been granted in the first place) or it may reverse the judgment and render judgment in the case for the losing party if no other evidence is necessary to a proper conclusion of the litigation, or it may partially affirm the judgment below and partially reverse it.

The attorney for the aggrieved party must decide for his client what is to be done next after any such judgment, as he made the decision for appeal following the judgment in the court below. In the appellate courts, it is a matter of law and its application to the evidence presented in the court below, and this must be handled by the attorneys in the case.

5. Lawsuits in the Workplace

At-Will Employment

No area of law has experienced greater change in recent years than employment law. Virtually every aspect of this area is now subject to federal and state regulation.

Most American workers are still "at-will" employees. This means they have no formal employment contract for a specific period of time. The employee serves at the will of the employer, and can be terminated—even without cause. But increasingly, there are limitations on this doctrine.

Some states have passed laws to protect all at-will employees from wrongful discharge. In these states, an employer must be prepared to show good cause for firing any employee. Other states have gone the opposite direction and codified the common law at-will doctrine. Texas has done neither. The common law doctrine is still recognized by the courts. At this time, the Texas Supreme Court has recognized only one exception: an employee cannot be fired for refusing to engage in illegal activities. But there are significant legislative exceptions which will be discussed in this chapter.

Legislative Exceptions to At-Will Employment

The Texas Whistleblower Act is an exception for all state or local governments. The law protects an employee who reports any violation of law. He or she cannot be fired or discriminated against for making such a report. If an employee is suspended or terminated within 90 days after making a report, there is a rebuttable presumption that the suspension or termination was retaliation. The alleged illegality does not have to be an actual violation; it is required only that the employee in good faith believes it is.

When a governmental agency violates the law, the employee is entitled to both actual and punitive damages. This statute has been interpreted broadly by the courts, and employees have won several large jury verdicts. When the defendant is the State of Texas, however, it may be difficult to collect the judgment. One cannot levy on a judgment against the state; the money must be appropriated by the legislature.

There have been discussions of a common-law whistleblower doctrine created by the courts; at this point, however, the Texas Supreme Court has not taken that step. Nevertheless, private employers should be cautious about firing people because they report what they in good faith believe are illegal actions by the company.

Of course, there are numerous federal statutes that punish employers who retaliate against whistleblowers. Examples are: The Railroad Safety Act, The Fair Labor Standards Act of 1938, the Occupational Safety and Health Act of 1970 (OSHA), and the civil rights statutes.

Equal Employment Opportunity

Equal Employment Opportunity (EEO) is a rapidly developing area of law. There are many new rights and remedies for employees. These laws can be a minefield for small businesses, which may have neither the time nor resources to understand and fully comply. Most of these laws have been around for years, but in the past, they had been enforced by injunctive relief such as reinstatement, promotion, and back pay. That has changed. There is now a pot of gold at the end of the rainbow.

The Civil Rights Act of 1991

The Civil Rights Act of 1991 amends Title VII of the Civil Rights Act of 1964 and other parts of equal opportunity legislation. Among other things, it provides money damages to employees who have been intentionally discriminated against under Title VII because of sex, religion, color, race, national origin, or disability under the Americans with Disabilities Act (ADA). The law applies to all employers "engaged in interstate commerce" with 15 or more employees. It also entitles employees to a jury trial if they allege intentional discrimination.

The law allows compensatory and punitive damages up to the following amounts, based on the size of the employer:

An employer with 15 to 100 employees:	$50,000
An employer with 101 to 200 employees:	$100,000
An employer with 201 to 500 employees:	$200,000
An employer with more than 500 employees:	$300,000

The law provides for additional punitive damages if the judge or jury finds that the employer acted with "malice or reckless indifference" to the employee's rights. All of this is in addition to traditional remedies such as reinstatement, back pay, and attorney's fees. And there is a bill before Congress now that would remove all caps on liability.

Title VII of The Civil Rights Act of 1964

Title VII of the Civil Rights Act of 1964 prohibits discrimination on the basis of race, color, religion, sex, age, disability, or national origin. An employer cannot use any of these categories to hire, fire, promote, compensate, classify, or in any way segregate employees that would tend to adversely affect the person's employee status. There is a major exception however: If any of these categories are a "bona fide occupational qualification" (BFOQ) reasonably necessary to the performance of a particular job, they can be used. Gender, for example, might, in some instances, be an essential job qualification. The same is true of religion—as in a denominational seminary.

Disparate Impact or Disparate Treatment

There are two different ways to violate the civil rights statutes: disparate treatment and disparate impact. Disparate treatment is the most common, and the easiest to prove. It involves a claim that an individual has been treated differently because of his or her membership in a protected class. The complainant must establish a *prima facie* case of discrimination.

In the employment context, this is done by proving: 1) membership in a protected class; 2) application for an available job; 3) evidence of qualifications for the job; 4) denial of the job; and 5) that the employer hired someone from another class, or continued to seek applicants for the position. If a *prima facie* case is established, the employer must defend by demonstrating that the action was based upon a legitimate, nondiscriminatory reason. The burden then shifts back to the complainant to show that the employer's reason is a pretext.

Disparate impact cases are more subtle. This is a claim by a group of people that certain employment rules or practices that appear neutral in reality have an adverse impact on that particular group or class of people. Standardized tests are a good example. Why should people who will be doing simple, manual tasks on an assembly line be required to pass a standardized test involving complex reading and math skills?

Historically, these tests tend to weed out minorities. Courts now require employers to demonstrate how such tests are justified by business necessity and are related to job performance.

Types of Discrimination Practices

Employers discriminate against employees in all kinds of ways. Supervisors are often unaware that long-established patterns of behavior may in fact be discriminatory, and may subject themselves and their company to a long, painful, and expensive lawsuit. This is a hard way to learn.

Overt racial or gender discrimination is rare today. Most people are aware of this aspect of the law. It would be unusual for a person to be told they are not being promoted because they are black, Hispanic, or female. But there are many subtle forms of discrimination. Often, factors may be involved from which one can legitimately infer that discrimination is the real reason. A judge or jury can look at the facts and draw their own conclusions.

One common form of discrimination is harassment. If the harassment is directed at an individual in a protected class because they are in that class, it may violate Title VII. Harassment can take the form of jokes, pranks, insults, vandalism, and other victim-directed behavior that becomes pervasive enough to form a "hostile" atmosphere. Being cute and funny at someone else's expense is no longer amusing. And it may be expensive.

Sexual Harassment

The most frequently litigated harassment today is sexual harassment. For most Americans, Anita Hill's testimony against

Supreme Court Justice Clarence Thomas dramatically underlined this area of law. The increased litigation probably indicates the pervasiveness of this behavior, and that is no longer being tolerated by a better informed workforce.

What is sexual harassment? In 1986, The United States Supreme Court described two types: 1) *quid pro quo* harassment, and 2) hostile environment harassment. *Quid pro quo* harassment occurs when submission to sexual advances is made either explicitly or implicitly, a term or condition of employment, or when a refusal to submit becomes the basis for a negative decision. Hostile environment harassment occurs when unwelcome, uninvited verbal or physical sexual advances or conduct become so pervasive that it alters the conditions of employment. It creates a hostile work environment.

In one classic old case, an elderly gentleman and his wife and son owned and operated a small dress factory. As long as they were all present, everything was fine. But when both his wife and son would leave, the old man would walk up and down the aisles patting the female workers on the buttocks and touching their breasts. His wife and son knew nothing, but must have wondered why there was such a rapid turnover of employees. The truth came out, however, when one of the women filed a complaint with the Equal Employment Opportunity Commission (EEOC). Since the old man was an owner and supervisor, the company was liable for damages.

The corporate risk of liability is greatest in a *quid pro quo* case. The higher the supervisor, the more likely it is that his actions will create vicarious liability for the company. This means the company is liable even if it didn't know what the supervisor was doing. It takes only one *quid pro quo* incident to create liability.

In 1998, the Supreme Court ruled that same-sex harassment is also a violation of the law. The Court further ruled that employers can be vicariously liable for both types of sexual harassment committed by lower-level supervisors if they had actual authority over employees. To successfully defend such a lawsuit, the company must show that it had sexual harassment procedures in place, that it had informed employees of those procedures, and that the complainant had failed to take advantage of those procedures.

Hostile environment liability requires a series of incidents. The company is not liable unless supervisors knew or should have known, and failed to act promptly to resolve the problem. Taking a "boys will be boys" approach is a certain path to liability.

At the same time, it must be remembered that political incorrectness is not the same thing as sexual harassment. Sexual harassment is victim directed, and it is based on gender. It is not necessarily male against female; a woman can be guilty of sexual harassment against a man. Gender is not the real key; the offense involves the use of a power relationship to sexually exploit another.

Sexual harassment applies also to students in public schools and universities. Students have a right to be free of sexual harassment from faculty and other students. In the case of *Franklin v. Gwinnet* (1993), the United States Supreme Court ruled for the first time that a public school district can be liable in money damages under Title IX. School administrators failed to act promptly when faced with evidence that a coach was sexually involved with a high school girl. Administrators finally accepted the coach's resignation, and persuaded the family not to file criminal charges. But it was too little, too late. This case is highly significant for schools. Failure to promptly investigate and resolve cases like this can create enormous liability against a school district. There is also a growing trend to hold districts liable for their failure to make reasonable efforts to protect students from the sexual abuse of other students.

Many companies and schools are offering training seminars on sexual harassment, along with other aspects of EEO law. Not only are employees less likely to violate the law when they are informed, but such programs can also be important to an institution's defense if charged with a violation.

Companies and schools should also include sexual harassment statements in policy manuals and employee handbooks. These efforts are not in vain. In August 1994, a San Francisco jury returned a verdict of $7.17 million in favor of a legal secretary against her former employer, a major law firm, and an ex-partner of the firm. A key part of the judgment grew out of the failure of the firm to discipline a successful and respected colleague, even though they were aware of his harassing behavior.

Pregnancy Discrimination Act

The Pregnancy Discrimination Act of 1978 is an amendment to Title VII. Under this law, an employer cannot treat a woman differently because she is pregnant or has had an abortion. Nor can an employment decision be based on marital status, unless it can be demonstrated that such status is a business necessity or a bona fide occupational qualification (BFOQ). The law can have unexpected applications. For example, jobs involving hazardous situations must be available to both men and women, regardless of the risks they might pose to pregnancy.

Perhaps the most significant impact is quite simple: An employer cannot force a pregnant woman to take sick leave if she is able to perform her duties. Nor can the employer deny any benefits because the pregnant employee is unmarried. Pregnancy must be treated just like any other job illness.

Family and Medical Leave Act of 1993

In 1993, the Family and Medical Leave Act was signed into law by President Bill Clinton. Its purpose is to protect employees who must take leaves of absence because of family or medical emergencies. The law covers only employers with 50 or more employees—about 50 percent of the American workforce.

The law appears simple enough, yet becomes surprisingly complex in application. The law requires employers to provide eligible employees with unpaid leave for up to 12 weeks for the birth or adoption of a child; the care of a seriously ill child, spouse, or parent; or the employee's own serious illness. To qualify, the employee must have worked for the employer for at least 12 months. The 12 weeks may be taken intermittently during a twelve-month period. In some circumstances, employers can require employees to use accrued sick leave or vacation time before the unpaid leave begins. It is in these areas that the law begins to get complex.

Religious Discrimination

Under Title VII, an employer cannot discriminate against an employee because of his or her religion. Religious harassment violates the law. It protects not only religious people; it covers atheists, as well. What does this mean? How far does it go? Completely apart from harassment, this law can present some unique problems. It does not require that an employer yield completely to an employee's religious convictions; he is required only to make a reasonable accommodation.

The problem usually arises when the job requires the employee to do something that violates his religious convictions. There have been lawsuits over whether an employee can be required to work on religious holidays. Can an individual be required to work on Saturday, for example, if his faith forbids work on the Sabbath? The answer is not easy.

The employer must "reasonably" accommodate the religious practice or conviction. He does not have to go so far, however, as to create "undue hardship" on the business. Undue hardship is interpreted as any significant cost or disruption. This will vary depending on the size and resources of a particular business. A small company that does most of its business on a Saturday might not have to accommodate. Being able to work on Saturday may be a BFOQ. It might be different for a large corporation. In this area, as in ADA cases, a willingness to be flexible is extremely important. Both employers and employees should try to work out creative solutions.

National Origin Discrimination

National Origin Discrimination is discrimination based on the place where a person or his or her ancestors were born. The Immigration and Control Act of 1986 prohibits hiring illegal aliens. A policy of hiring United States citizens does not violate the law. But such a policy must not be used as a pretext for discrimination.

This kind of discrimination usually occurs because of a person's appearance, accent, or dress. Sometimes it is a result of international conflicts; many citizens from Iran experienced this during the Iranian crisis in the late 1970s. English language proficiency requirements are illegal unless the job itself calls for communication skills. Courts routinely strike down English-only workplace rules, unless the employer can show a business necessity for them. Ethnic jokes and slurs are a type of harassment that can be illegal if pervasive in the workplace.

Equal Pay Act of 1963

The Equal Pay Act of 1963 prohibits an employer from using gender as the basis for paying employees different salaries or compensation for equal work. The statute is an amendment to the Fair Labor Standards Act. Both men and women are protected. Men and women must receive equal pay for equal work if they work in the same establishment, the work requires similar skills, and the work is performed under similar conditions.

There are exceptions, however. Differences attributed to a bona fide seniority system or legitimate merit raises are acceptable. Pay differences attributed to quantity or quality of production are legal. A company can use other reasons to defend differences as long as they are valid and are not based on gender.

Unlike Title VII cases, a complainant can file directly in court without going through the EEOC. Damages, however, are limited to back pay, attorneys' fees, and court costs. A complainant has two years after the incident to sue for nonwillful violations, and three years for willful violations. Damages may be doubled if the violations are found to be willful.

Americans with Disabilities Act of 1990

The Americans with Disabilities Act (ADA) was signed into law by President George Bush in July 1990. It is the strongest mandate in the nation's history to eliminate discrimination against the disabled. The law deals with four areas: employment (Title I), public services (Title II), public accommodation (Title III), and telecommunications (Title IV). It is a complex statute; only Title I, affecting employment law, will be discussed here.

The law covers government agencies, as well as all private employers engaged in a business or industry affecting interstate commerce, who have 15 or more employees. Employers with 15 or more employees not covered by the interstate commerce provisions of the federal law are probably subject to the Texas Employment Discrimination statute (Section 21, Labor Code). This statute requires only that the business be engaged "in an industry affecting commerce." One of the stated purposes of the Texas law is to execute "the policies embodied in Title I of the Americans with Disabilities Act of 1990." The law is enforced by the EEOC and the Texas Human Rights Commission.

The purposes of the law are laudable. It is intended to give the disabled new opportunities for participation in the marketplace and to assist them in achieving self-sufficiency. Many employers are indeed discovering that the disabled are often among their most productive employees.

But the law has problems, both in interpretation and enforcement. In the first place, it is drawn broadly. Who are the disabled? According to the statute, to be "disabled," a person must fall into at least one of these categories: 1) He or she must have a physical or mental impairment that substantially limits one or more major life activities; 2) He or she must have a record of such impairment; or 3) He or she must be regarded as having such an impairment. Some observers have estimated that at least 43 million Americans are covered by this statute.

The law covers such things as orthopedic impairments, mental retardation, mental illness, cancer, speech disorders, sight and hearing impairments, diabetes, AIDS, severe obesity, cosmetic disfigurements, addiction to lawful drugs, and hundreds of other significant diseases and conditions. The key question is: Does it "substantially" limit a "major life activity?"

The law does not apply to trivial or temporary illnesses, impairments resulting from cultural or economic disadvantages, or gender and identity disorders. Homosexuality is excluded, as is the current use of alcohol or illegal drugs. Recovered alcoholics or users of legal drugs, however, are protected by the ADA. Compulsive gambling, kleptomania, and pyromania are not covered.

All of this does not require an employer to hire every disabled person who applies for work. The individual must be a "qualified individual with a disability." This means the disabled person must be able to perform all essential functions of the job, with or without reasonable accommodation. One is not required to hire people who can't do the job. An employer, however, should be able to distinguish essential from non-essential job functions. And the employer must be willing to make reasonable accommodations to enable an individual to perform the essential functions of the job.

What must an employer do to reasonably accommodate a disabled employee? Here again, the law is vague. The employer must accommodate, but is not required to incur "undue hardship." What is undue hardship? It depends on the cost or inconvenience of the accommodation, and the resources of the employer. It must be decided on a case-by-case basis. This obviously provides little guidance to businesses trying to comply with the law.

The best approach probably involves common sense and creativity. Most accommodations are inexpensive. Asking for suggestions from the disabled employee can help. Being negative and inflexible is the worst approach. And it will probably cost more in the long run. Litigation is expensive.

The ADA has had a major impact on hiring procedures. There are certain questions that simply cannot be asked. An interviewer cannot ask about the disability or how it was incurred. A pre-employment medical examination can be required after a job offer has been made, but not before. This area is too specialized to cover here. Information about proper hiring procedures is widely available; business owners and managers should make sure they have access to this information.

Litigation concerning ADA is increasing. Good information and common sense, however, can go a long way toward keeping a person out of court.

Age Discrimination In Employment Act of 1967

The Age Discrimination in Employment Act was passed to protect employees 40 or older from discrimination based on age. It applies to all terms and conditions of employment. For the most part, it forbids mandatory retirement at any age. It does allow for the mandatory retirement at age 65 of bona fide executives, or those in high, policy-making positions, if they have held their position for two years immediately preceding retirement, and are entitled to retirement income of at least $44,000 per year.

There are other exceptions. In some situations, age may be a bona fide occupational qualification—as with firefighters and police officers. Bona fide employee benefit plans are also an exception. And of course age is no defense when one is being disciplined for poor job performance.

Employee Polygraph Protection Act of 1988

The Employee Polygraph Protection Act makes it illegal for employers to require employees or job applicants to submit to a lie detector test. The law resulted from the widespread misuse of this investigative tool. It can still be used, however, if there is reasonable suspicion that an employee was involved in a theft or other illegal activity.

EEOC Enforcement Procedure

Any person who believes he or she has a valid complaint may file a charge with the EEOC or the Texas Commission on Human Rights. The charge must be in writing and identify the name and address of the complaining party. It must name the offending organization and the number of its employees, if known. It should include a brief statement of facts. It may be filed at any EEOC field office, the state agency, or with headquarters in Washington. The agency is liberal in accepting charges. If the original statement is incomplete, it will ask for additional information.

In states where there is no local fair employment practices agency, the complaint must be filed within 180 days of the alleged violation. If there is a state agency (as in Texas), the filing time is extended to 300 days—although in reality it is only 240 days, since the state agency must be given 60 days to consider the complaint.

Within 10 days after receiving a charge, the EEOC must notify the employer of the allegations. The employer has an opportunity to respond. The EEOC then has several choices. It can do a full formal investigation, issue subpoenas, hold hearings, and compel people to testify. Or it can investigate informally. It can seek a conciliation agreement. It can file a lawsuit, or decide not to sue, in which case it will issue a "right to sue" letter to the complainant.

Once a complainant receives a "right to sue" letter, he or she has only 90 days in which to file suit. Once suit is filed, the case proceeds into state or federal court as with any other litigation.

This survey is only an overview. Not all of the relevant statutes have been discussed. This area of law is complex and rapidly changing, and it has a very direct effect on the lives of most citizens of this state.

6. The Texas Penal Code

The Texas Legislature of 1973 adopted a new Penal Code that became effective on January 1, 1974. Prior to this action, much groundwork and drafting had been done by a committee appointed by the board of directors of the State Bar Association of Texas, a committee appointed by the Texas District and County Attorneys Association, and a committee appointed by the Texas Criminal Defense Lawyers Association. The result was a great improvement over the old code, which had been disorganized and confusing.

In 1991, the legislature abolished the 1973 code effective September 1, 1994 and created the Texas Punishments Standards Commission to rewrite the Penal Code and propose procedural changes. After public hearings and an examination of the entire code, the commission recommended extensive changes, most of which were adopted by the 1993 legislature. The new Penal Code went into effect on September 1, 1994. In most respects, it is a revision of the 1973 code, but there are significant differences.

Objectives and Philosophy of the Code

The purpose of our criminal law is clearly stated in the statute itself. That purpose is to establish a system of prohibitions, penalties, and correctional measures to deal with conduct that threatens harm to individual or public interests. It postulates the goal of the criminal justice system as: to ensure the public safety through (a) the deterrent influence of the penalties provided, (b) the rehabilitation of those convicted of violations of the code, and (c) such punishment as may be necessary to prevent likely recurrence of criminal behavior.

Statutory Law

Some jurisdictions recognize common-law crimes. These are crimes recognized and defined by the courts rather than the legislature. This is not true in Texas. Conduct is not criminal unless it is so defined by statute, municipal ordinance, order of a commissioner's court or by rules authorized by statute.

Burden of Proof

As under prior law, the new code provides that all persons are presumed innocent, and no person may be convicted of an offense unless each element of the offense is proved beyond a reasonable doubt. Guilt cannot be inferred from the fact that a person has been arrested, confined, or indicted for the offense.

A Voluntary Act

Under the code, a person commits an offense only when he voluntarily engages in conduct, including an act, an omission, or possession. Possession is a voluntary act if the possessor knowingly receives the object, or is aware of his control of the thing for a sufficient time to permit him to terminate his control.

Suppose a person is walking along a street and has a seizure. In falling to the ground, he slings his arm around and strikes and injures a bystander with his umbrella. No one would argue that he should be charged with the crime of assault; it is obvious that his conduct was not a voluntary act.

An omission to act is not an offense unless a statute provides that it is, or otherwise provides that a person has a duty to perform the act. Failure to stop and render aid after being involved in an automobile accident is a good example of an omission that is a violation of law.

Culpable Mental States

The code defines the mental element (*mens rea,* as it is often called) necessary to establish a particular crime. The code sets out four culpable mental states: intentional, knowing, reckless, and criminal negligence.

The most serious of these mental states is the *intentional* act. A person acts intentionally when it is his conscious objective to engage in the conduct or cause the result. Usually, a person's intent can be inferred from his actions. When a person picks up a gun and fires three shots at another person, his intent is obvious. We would reach another conclusion, though, if he fired the three shots into the air.

The next level of offense is the *knowing* act. A person acts knowingly when he is aware of the nature of his conduct, or that the circumstances exist, and that his conduct is reasonably certain to cause the result. For example, a person might be guilty of receiving stolen property, where even though he did not "know" the property was stolen (i.e., the facts of the theft), he nevertheless "knew" of enough circumstances to cause a reasonable person to be aware that the goods were stolen. The line between "intentional" and "knowing" acts is thin.

The third level of culpability is *reckless*. This occurs when a person is aware, but consciously disregards a substantial and unjustifiable risk that the circumstances exist, or the result will occur. The risk must be of such a nature that its disregard constitutes a gross deviation from the standard of care than an ordinary person would exercise under all the circumstances as viewed from the actor's viewpoint.

The lowest level of culpability is *criminal negligence.* One is guilty of this when he ought to be aware of a substantial and unjustifiable risk that the circumstances exist or the result will occur. The risk must be of such a degree that the failure to perceive it constitutes a gross deviation from the standard of care that an ordinary person would exercise under all the circumstances as viewed from the actor's standpoint. This is more than ordinary negligence, as required to establish a civil negligence case. The Texas Court of Criminal Appeals has overturned a municipal ordinance making "negligent collision" a traffic offense, because the standard set was simple, not gross, negligence. In Texas, simple negligence cannot be the basis of a criminal charge.

From these definitions, it should be obvious that the task of determining the degree of culpability in a specific situation can be difficult. This is the challenge to the factfinder in a case—usually the jury.

Classifications of Offenses and Punishments

Under the old law, the classification of offenses and punishments was complex and confusing; each offense had its own punishment written into the statute. This had been simplified and systemized in the new code, and continues in the revision.

Offenses fall into two classifications: *felonies,* which are punishable by sentence to the penitentiary or by death; and *misdemeanors,* which are punishable by jail sentences, fines, or both.

Classification of Felonies

Felonies are classified into five categories according to the relative seriousness of the offense:

1. Capital felonies, punishable by death or life imprisonment
2. Felonies of the first degree, punishable by confinement in the penitentiary for a term not less than five, and up to life or ninety-nine years, with a possible fine not to exceed $10,000
3. Felonies of the second degree, punishable by confinement in the penitentiary for a term of not less than two years nor more than twenty years, and a possible fine not to exceed $10,000
4. Felonies of the third degree, punishable by confinement in the penitentiary for a term of not less than two years nor more than ten years, with a possible fine not to exceed $10,000
5. State jail felonies, punishable by confinement in a state jail for not less than 180 days nor more than two years

Classification of Misdemeanors

Misdemeanors are classified into three classifications according to the seriousness of the offense:

1. Class A misdemeanors, punishable by a fine of not more than $4,000 or confinement in jail for a term not to exceed one year, or both
2. Class B misdemeanors, punishable by a fine of not more than $2,000 or confinement in jail for a term not to exceed six months, or both
3. Class C misdemeanors, punishable by a fine of not more than $500

Defenses to Criminal Responsibility

Although an individual has committed a criminal act, the law recognizes certain situations or conditions that should excuse or mitigate the usual punishment. Though people sometimes say there is never an excuse for crimes, as they serve on juries and see specific fact situations, they do recognize and apply these defenses.

Insanity

The new code brought a substantial difference to the law defining insanity as a defense to a criminal act. Prior law was based on the old M'Naughten rule: The defendant was excused if his mental defect was so severe, that either he did not know what he was doing, or if he did know, he did not know that it was wrong.

Under the new code, the defendant had a defense if, as a result of mental disease or defect: (a) he did not know his conduct was wrong, or (b) he was incapable of conforming his conduct to the law he allegedly violated. In 1983, however, the legislature amended the code by removing the second clause, in effect returning Texas to the "right-wrong" or M'Naughten rule.

Lay people often think that insanity is a gimmick frequently used by criminals to "get off the hook." In fact, it is not a popular plea among those accused of crime, and is not particularly successful when pled.

Mistake of Fact

The penal code states that it is a defense to prosecution that the actor, through mistake, formed a reasonable belief about a matter of fact, if his mistaken belief negated the kind of culpability required for commission of the offense.

Suppose a lady is walking along a street and sees a package fall out of a moving automobile. She walks over and picks it up, and is trying to decide what to do, when an officer arrives and takes her and the package into custody. Later, it is determined that the package contained heroin. The lady certainly "possessed" the package, but she is not guilty of the crime of possession of heroin.

Mistake of Law

It is frequently stated that "ignorance of the law is no excuse." The penal code provides that it is no defense to prosecution that the person is ignorant of or mistaken about the law under which he is being prosecuted. In certain situations, however, his ignorance can serve as a basis for mitigation of punishment. It is also a defense that a person believes his conduct is legal because is relying on an official statement or interpretation of law by an agency, court, or official with the responsibility to interpret that law.

Intoxication

Texas law is very strict in its prohibition against voluntary intoxication as a defense to crime. It is never a defense. For example, a person can be convicted of theft, even though at the time of the taking, he was so drunk that he could not possibly have been aware of his act and the surrounding circumstances.

If a person is so drunk that he is "temporarily insane," that fact can be used to mitigate his punishment.

Duress

A person has a defense if he engages in illegal conduct because he was compelled to do so by threat of imminent death or serious bodily injury to himself or another. What is compulsion? The penal code defines it as "force or threat of force (that) would render a person of reasonable firmness incapable of resisting the pressure" (Art. 8.05). Just what this means in a particular case must be determined by the judge or jury.

Entrapment

Entrapment occurs when a person is induced to violate the law by a law enforcement agent. One who merely takes advantage of an opportunity provided by police is not entrapped. The question is whether the action of the police would have been likely to induce one with innocent intentions to commit a crime: Did they actually implant a criminal design in the mind of the defendant? This, of course, is the defense raised in many police and FBI "sting" operations.

Justification

In certain situations, acts that would be otherwise classified as criminal are not so classified because they are considered justified. A good example is self-defense. The law recognizes that a person is justified in using force against another to the extent he reasonably believes it is "immediately necessary" to protect himself against the unlawful use of force by the other person. He can only use that degree of force that is necessary to protect himself, i.e., he can use deadly force to protect against deadly force, but not against a lesser threat.

A person has a right to use force, sometimes even deadly force, to protect his property. One is certainly justified in using a deadly weapon to repel a burglar from his home. Texans, however, are now more restricted in the use of deadly force than under prior law. One cannot shoot a mere trespasser on his land, when he presents no threat.

Criminal Attempt, Conspiracy, and Riot

Criminal Attempt

Criminal attempt punishes conduct falling short of the completed offense. A person commits the offense if, with specific intent, he does an act amounting to more than "mere preparation," but fails to commit the offense intended.

For example, a man who holds a grudge against a police officer makes up his mind to murder him and takes his gun and draws a bead on the officer and fires his gun, but his aim is poor and the other person is not hit by the bullet. He actually intended and attempted to commit the offense, but his efforts failed. If his efforts had succeeded, he could have been prosecuted for a capital felony, but because his efforts failed, he could be prosecuted and convicted for an offense one category lower than the intended offense, in this case a first-degree felony.

The same rule holds for attempts to commit offenses of lower degree. The actor or offender can be prosecuted for an offense one category lower than the offense he intended to commit.

Criminal Conspiracy

A person commits criminal conspiracy if, with intent that a felony be committed:

1. He agrees with one or more persons that they or one or more of them engage in conduct that would constitute the offense; or
2. He or one or more of them performs an overt act in pursuance of the agreement.

Under the prior statute, it was necessary to prove an actual agreement between two or more parties before there could be a successful prosecution. Under the present statute, there does not have to be a genuine agreement. It is necessary only that the party to be prosecuted agrees. The other party may be an undercover agent with no intent of carrying out the purported agreement. The co-conspirators can be prosecuted for the offense one category lower than the offense which they agreed to commit.

Riot

As under the conspiracy statute, one who participates in a "riot" may incur criminal liability for the actions of someone else. A riot is defined as an "assemblage of seven or more persons" resulting in conduct that creates an immediate danger to property or persons, obstructs law enforcement or other governmental functions or services, or by force or threat of force deprives any person of a legal right. The problem is that anyone in the "riot" may be convicted of a greater offense committed by another participant in the riot if: (a) the criminal act was in furtherance of the purpose of the assembly, or (b) it was an offense that should have been anticipated as a result of the assembly.

For example, suppose a group of 50 parents assembled at a school, angry because of a federal busing order. The situation gets rowdy, and one of the parents shoots and kills a bus driver. It is possible for the other 49 to be tried and convicted of murder, even though they had no intent for the crime to occur.

Punishment of Corporations or Associations

A corporation or association is a "legal entity," but it is not susceptible to being put in prison. If it is convicted of an offense, its punishment has to be by fine. If it is convicted of an offense for which a fine is provided, its punishment is the fine provided for the offense of which it is convicted. If under the law the offense is a felony of whatever category or degree, the court may fix a fine not to exceed $20,000. If the offense is a Class A or Class B misdemeanor, the fine is any amount fixed by the court not to exceed $10,000. If it is a Class C misdemeanor, the fine will not exceed $2,000. If, as a result of an offense classified as a felony or Class A misdemeanor, an individual suffers serious bodily injury or death, a fine of up to $50,000 can be imposed. If the court finds that the offense committed by the corporation or association resulted in financial gain to the offender, in lieu of the fines otherwise provided, the court may assess a fine of any amount not to exceed twice the amount of the gain.

Offenses Against the Person

With the foregoing general provisions and definitions in mind, we turn now to the several groups of offenses that are made punishable by law, the first and most serious being offenses against the person.

Capital Murder

A capital offense is one for which a person can receive the death penalty. In the 1972 decision of *Furman v. Georgia,* the United States Supreme Court ruled that in the circumstances of those cases, the death penalty was unconstitutional. Only two justices were of the opinion that it was, per se, cruel and unusual punishment. The majority hinted that the death penalty might be valid if not "arbitrarily and wantonly" imposed.

Following this decision, 35 states and the federal government revised their capital punishment statutes in an attempt to eliminate these constitutional problems. Texas was one of these. The Texas statute provides that the death penalty may be assessed only if a person knowingly and intentionally causes the death of another, and

1. The person murdered is a peace officer or fireman in the lawful discharge of an official duty, and the person knows this fact;

2. The person intentionally commits the murder in the course of committing or attempting to commit kidnapping, burglary, robbery, aggravated rape, or arson;

3. The person commits the murder for remuneration or the promise of remuneration or employs another to commit the murder for remuneration or the promise of remuneration;

4. The person commits the murder while escaping or attempting to escape from a penal institution;

5. The person, while incarcerated in a penal institution, murders another who is employed in the operation of a penal institution, or murders another person as a part of a combination;

6. The person commits murder while incarcerated for murder, capital murder, or while serving a life sentence for aggravated kidnapping, aggravated sexual assault, or aggravated robbery;

7. The person murders more than one person during the same criminal transaction or pursuant to the same scheme or course of conduct; or

8. The person murders an individual under six years of age.

If a defendant is found guilty by a jury of one of these offenses, then the judge must conduct a separate sentencing hearing before the jury to determine whether the defendant shall be sentenced to death or life imprisonment.

Before a defendant can be assessed the death penalty for a murder committed after September 1, 1991, there must be a finding by the jury that

(a) There is a probability that the defendant would commit acts of violence that would constitute a continuing threat to society, and

(b) In cases where the defendant was found guilty as a party, the defendant actually caused the death of the deceased or if he did not, he intended to kill the deceased or another or anticipated that a human life would be taken.

If the jury answers both of these questions in the affirmative, a third question must be submitted: "Whether, taking into consideration all of the evidence, including the circumstances of the offense, the defendant's character and background, and the personal moral culpability of the defendant, there is a sufficient mitigating circumstance or circumstances to warrant that a sentence of life imprisonment rather than a death sentence be imposed."

If the murder was committed prior to September, 1991, there must be a finding by the jury that

(a) The defendant's conduct was committed deliberately and with the reasonable expectation that the death of the deceased would result;

(b) That there is a probability that the defendant would be a continuing threat to society; and

(c) If there was any provocation by the deceased, that the defendant's response to that provocation was unreasonable.

Ironically, under our present law, that form of murder traditionally regarded as the most serious, the calculated, intentional, premeditated murder of another human being, is no longer punishable by death. If a man hires someone to kill his wife, he is subject to the death penalty. But if he lays his plot and commits the murder himself, the most he can receive is life imprisonment. The Supreme Court subsequently ruled that the death penalty assessed under this and similar state statutes is constitutional.

Murder (Less than Capital)

Murder is defined as intentionally or knowingly causing the death of an individual. A person also commits the offense if he intends to cause serious bodily injury and commits an act clearly dangerous to human life that causes the death of an individual. It is also murder if one commits or attempts to commit a felony and in the course of his actions, or in flight therefrom, he attempts or commits an act clearly dangerous to human life that causes the death of an individual. This offense is a felony of the first degree, punishable by life imprisonment or a sentence of not less than five nor more than 95 years.

Second-Degree Murder

As of September 1, 1994, the old offense of voluntary manslaughter is no longer a separate offense. It has been replaced with second-degree murder. If the defendant proves he acted "under the immediate influence of sudden passion arising from an adequate cause," during the punishment phase he is entitled to receive the sentence for a second-degree felony. What is sudden passion?

The statute defines it as "passion directly caused by and arising out of provocation by the individual killed or another person acting with him." *Adequate cause* is that which would commonly produce a degree of anger, rage, resentment, or terror in a person of ordinary temper, sufficient to render the mind incapable of cool reflection. The difficult task of applying these definitions to specific situations is the task of the judge or jury. Second-degree murder is a lesser included offense of murder.

Manslaughter

A person may be charged with manslaughter if he recklessly causes the death of an individual. This offense has been simplified. It is a felony of the second degree.

Evidence

In the trial of cases of murder or voluntary manslaughter, the state and defendant are permitted to offer testimony to show any and all facts about the circumstances surrounding the killing and the prior relationship of the person accused and the deceased. Defense attorneys sometimes "try the deceased" and so enrage the jury that they not only find the defendant not guilty, they want to "dig up the deceased and kill him again." This does not always work however, and can boomerang and hurt the defedant's case.

Whether or not the defendant should testify is frequently a close question. He or she is not required to do so, and the jury will be instructed to not consider this as a factor. Most jurors nevertheless expect to hear the defendant's explanation for the accusations against him or her.

Criminally Negligent Homicide

A person commits a state jail felony if he causes the death of another by criminal negligence.

Kidnapping and False Imprisonment

One commits the offense of false imprisonment if he intentionally or knowingly restrains another person without his consent, so as to interfere substantially with his liberty. This offense is a Class B misdemeanor, unless it exposes the victim to a substantial risk of serious bodily injury, in which case it is a felony of the third degree. It is an affirmative defense against prosecution, however, if the person restrained was a child of less than 14 years of age, and the actor was a relative of the child, whose sole intent was to assume lawful control of the child.

The offense of kidnapping occurs when a person intentionally abducts another person. An abduction occurs when a person is restrained by (a) secreting him in a place where he is not likely to be found, or (b) using or threatening to use deadly force. It is a defense that the actor was a relative of the person abducted, and his sole intent was to assume lawful control of the victim. Kidnapping is a felony of the third degree.

Aggravated kidnapping is a felony of the first degree. It occurs when the actor abducts another person with the intent to

(a) Hold him or her for ransom;
(b) Use him or her as a shield or hostage;
(c) Facilitate the commission of a felony or the flight therefrom;
(d) Inflict bodily injury or violate or abuse him or her sexually;
(e) Terrorize him or her or a third person; or
(f) Interfere with the performance of any governmental or political function.

The law seeks to encourage the actor to release his victims alive in a safe place by providing that if he does so, the offense is only a felony of the second degree.

Sexual Offenses

Sexual Assault

The offense formerly known as "rape" is now covered under the statute prohibiting "sexual assault." Sexual assault is defined as the "penetration of the anus or female sexual organ of another person by any means without that person's consent." Marriage is no longer a defense. One can be found guilty of sexually assaulting his own spouse while they are married and still living together. The act is without one's consent in the following situations:

(a) The actor compels the other person to submit by the use of physical force or violence;
(b) The actor threatens to use force or violence against someone and the other person believes the actor has the present ability to execute the threat;
(c) The other person has not consented and is unconscious or physically unable to resist;

(d) The actor knows that because of a mental disease or defect the other person is unable to appraise the situation;

(e) The other person has not consented and the actor knows the person is unaware that sexual assault is occurring;

(f) The actor has intentionally impaired the other person's control by administering any substance without his knowledge;

(g) The actor compels the other to submit by threatening to use force or violence against any person, and the victim believes he has the ability to execute the threat;

(h) The actor is a public servant who coerced the person to submit.

(i) The actor is a mental health provider who ". . . exploits the other's emotional dependency." This is so even though the sexual relationship is in fact between consenting adults; or

(j) The actor is a clergyman who ". . . exploits the other's emotional dependency." As in the above paragraph, consent of the victim is no defense even though he or she is a competent adult.

Sexual assault is a felony of the second degree, unless it is aggravated sexual assault in which case it is a felony of the first degree. Aggravated sexual assault occurs when the actor achieves his purpose by either threatening or causing kidnapping, serious bodily injury, or death to the victim or another in the course of the criminal episode.

When a person has been charged with sexual assault, his attorney can question the victim about previous sexual conduct and reputation only if the judge finds that the evidence is material to a fact at issue in the case, and that its inflammatory or prejudicial nature does not outweigh its probative value.

Sexual Abuse

The law describes various sex abuses including deviate or abnormal sex activity and sets the penalties for their commission. Such acts are felonies when committed against or with a child. There is no punishment when these acts are carried on between husband and wife as long as they are consensual. Homosexual conduct is now a Class C misdemeanor.

Sexual Assault of a Child

It is a felony of the second degree if a person intentionally commits any of the following actions with a person under the age of 17 (a child) who is not his spouse:

(a) Penetration of the anus or female sex organ of the child by any means;
(b) Penetration of the mouth by the sexual organ of the actor; or
(c) Causing the sexual organ of the child to contact or penetrate the mouth, anus, or sexual organ of another person.

It is a defense if the actor is not more than three years older than the victim. Promiscuity of the child is no longer a defense. If a child is younger than 14, it is the first-degree felony of aggravated sexual assault. Consent is no defense.

Indecency with a Child

Indecency with a child is a second-degree felony if it involves "sexual contact" with a child younger than 17 who is not the spouse of the actor. It is a third-degree felony if one exposes his anus or any part of his genitals knowing the child is present, with intent to arouse or satisfy the sexual desire of any person.

"Sexual contact" means any touching of the anus, breast, or any part of the genitals of another person with intent to arouse or gratify the sexual desire of any person. It is a defense to the charge if the accused is not more than three years older than the victim, and did not use force, duress, or a threat. The former defense of "promiscuity" on the part of the minor has been eliminated.

Assaultive Offenses

Assault

A person commits an offense if he

1. Intentionally, knowingly, or recklessly causes bodily injury to another, including the actor's spouse;
2. Intentionally or knowingly threatens another with imminent bodily injury, including the actor's spouse; or
3. Intentionally or knowingly causes physical contact with another when he knows or should reasonably believe that the other will regard the contact as offensive or provocative.

These offenses are misdemeanors unless they are against a public servant discharging an official duty, in which case they are third-degree felonies.

Aggravated Assault

If in committing assault, as described above, the actor

1. Causes serious bodily injury to another; or
2. Uses or exhibits a deadly weapon during the assault, he is guilty of a felony of the second degree.

It is a felony of the first degree if it is committed by a public servant under color of the servant's office, if it is against a public servant lawfully discharging an official duty, or if it is in retaliation against a witness who has reported the occurrence of a crime.

Injury to a Child or an Elderly or Disabled Individual

A person commits a felony if he intentionally, knowingly, or recklessly by omission causes serious bodily injury, serious physical or mental deficiency or impairment, or bodily injury to a child who is 14 years of age or younger, or to a person who is 65 years of age or older. If the conduct was done negligently or recklessly and caused only bodily injury (not serious bodily injury), it is a state jail felony.

Abandoning or Endangering a Child

It is a state jail felony to leave a child in any place without providing reasonable care under circumstances where no reasonable adult would leave a child of that age and ability, or to abandon the child in any place that exposes him or her to an unreasonable risk of harm. It is a second-degree felony if the actor abandons the child in circumstances that place it in imminent danger of death, bodily injury, or physical or mental impairment.

A person who leaves a child younger than seven alone in a motor vehicle for longer than five minutes has committed a Class C misdemeanor.

Deadly Conduct

A person commits a third-degree felony or Class A misdemeanor if he recklessly engages in conduct that places another in imminent danger of serious bodily injury, for example pointing a gun at another whether or not the actor believes the gun to be loaded.

Terroristic Threat

A person commits an offense if he threatens to commit any offense involving violence to any person or property with intent to

1. Cause a reaction of any type to his threat by an official or volunteer agency organized to deal with emergencies;
2. Place any person in fear of imminent serious bodily injury;
3. Prevent or interrupt the occupation or use of a building, room, place of assembly, place to which the public has access, place of employment or occupation, aircraft, automobile, or other form of conveyance, or other public place; or
4. Cause impairment or interruption of public communication; public transportation; public water, gas, or power supply; or other public source.

Offenses Against the Family

Bigamy

If a person is legally married and he

(a) Purports to marry or does marry a person other than his spouse in this state, or any other state or foreign country, under circumstances that would, but for the actor's prior marriage, constitute a marriage; or
(b) Lives with a person other than his spouse in this state under the appearance of being married,

then he has committed a "Class A" misdemeanor.

If a person is legally married and knows that a married person other than his spouse is married and he

(a) Purports to marry or does marry that person in this state, or any other state or foreign country, under circumstances that would, but for the person's prior marriage, constitute a marriage; or

(b) Lives with that person in this state under the appearance of being married

he also commits a Class A misdemeanor.

It is a defense to prosecution under the first provision above that the actor reasonably believed that his marriage was void or had been dissolved by death, divorce, or annulment.

A lawful wife or husband of the actor may testify both for and against the actor concerning proof of the original marriage, and this includes a common-law spouse.

Prohibited Sexual Conduct

A person commits a felony of the third degree if he engages in sexual intercourse or deviate sexual intercourse with a person he knows to be, without regard to legitimacy:

1. An ancestor or descendant by blood or adoption;
2. His stepchild or stepparent, while the marriage creating the relationship exists;
3. His parent's brother or sister of the whole or half blood;
4. His brother or sister of the whole or half blood or by adoption; or
5. The children of his brother or sister of the whole or half blood or by adoption.

Interference with Child Custody

A person commits an offense if he takes or retains a child younger than 18 years out of the county or counties composing the judicial district of the appropriate court, when he

1. Knows that his taking or retention violates a temporary or permanent judgment or order of a court disposing of the child's custody; or

2. Has not been awarded custody of the child by a court of competent jurisdiction and knows that a suit for divorce, or civil suit or application for habeas corpus to dispose of the child's custody, has been filed, and he intends to deprive the court of authority.

It is a defense to (2) above that the actor returned the child to this state within three days from the date of commission of the offense. An offense under these provisions is a state jail felony. This new provision is intended to fill a gap or hiatus in the law that has long been a frustration to parents, attorneys, judges, and law enforcement officers.

Now, when the relationship between parents reaches the state where a court must decide between them, the one not awarded custody of the child will do well to leave the physical custody of the child where the court places it. It is taking the child out of the jurisdiction of the court that makes the offense so serious.

It is a Class B misdemeanor to interfere knowingly and intentionally with the custody of a child under 18 years of age by enticing it from the custody of the parent or guardian or the person standing in the stead of the parent or guardian.

Violation of Protective Order

It is a Class A misdemeanor to violate a "protective order" issued by a court or to commit "family violence" in violation of the Family Code. This statute puts teeth into the law and authorizes police to intervene in family law situations that they used to avoid.

Criminal Nonsupport

A person commits a state jail felony if he intentionally or knowingly fails to provide support that he can provide and that he is legally obligated to provide for his children younger than 18 years. A child includes one born out of wedlock whose paternity has been acknowledged by the father or established by the court.

Harboring a Runaway Child

A person commits a Class A misdemeanor if he knowingly harbors a child and is "criminally negligent" about whether the child is younger than 18 years, and the child has escaped from the custody of a peace officer, or probation officer or the Texas Youth Council, or is voluntarily absent from the child's home without consent of the parent or guardian for a substantial length of time without the intent to return. It is a defense if the actor is related to the child within the second degree by consanguinity or affinity, or that he notified a law enforcement agency within 24 hours after discovering the child's status.

Having dealt with offenses against the person and the family, we now turn to offenses against property, which can also carry heavy penalties.

Offenses Against Property

Criminal Mischief

A person commits criminal mischief if, without the owner's consent, he intentionally or knowingly damages or destroys the tangible property of the owner, or tampers with the property and causes pecuniary loss or substantial inconvenience. It is also a violation to make markings, inscriptions, paintings, or slogans on another's property. The punishment ranges from a Class C misdemeanor to a felony of the first degree, depending on the amount of the loss or damage.

Robbery

A person commits a felony of the second degree if, in the course of committing theft and with intent to obtain or maintain control of the property, he

1. Intentionally, knowingly, or recklessly causes bodily injury to another; or
2. Intentionally or knowingly threatens or places another in fear of imminent bodily injury or death.

Robbery generally involves taking property from the person or possession of another, and it is often associated with violence. If the robber causes serious bodily injury to another or uses or exhibits a deadly weapon, the offense is a felony of the first degree. This is known as aggravated robbery.

Burglary

If, without the consent of the owner, a person goes into or remains concealed in a habitation or building not then open to the public and attempts to commit a felony or theft, he commits burglary, which is a state jail felony. It is a felony of the second degree if the building is a habitation. It is not necessary that the one committing the crime enter the habitation or building with his whole body. He may reach in with an arm or hand or poke through a window or other opening a fishing pole or other object to retrieve the objects he is trying to steal, and he commits the offense. Moreover, if the premises entered are a habitation, and any party to the offense entered the habitation with intent to commit a felony other than felony theft, the offense is a felony of the first degree.

Burglary of Vehicles

One who breaks into a vehicle with intent to commit a felony or theft commits a Class A misdemeanor. The breaking in may be into any part of the vehicle, the trunk or the main body of it, and vehicle in this sense means automobiles, trucks, enclosed tractors, road graders, a vessel, steamboat, or railroad car.

Theft

The offense of theft has several elements: intending to deprive the owner of property, obtaining possession of it, or exercising control of it (other than real estate), unlawfully. Thus, a person who receives or conceals stolen property is guilty of theft the same as the one who steals it originally.

The offense is

1. A Class C misdemeanor if the value of the property stolen is less than $50;
2. A Class B misdemeanor if
   a. the value of the property stolen is $50 or more but less than $500;
   b. the value of the property stolen is less than $50 and the defendant has previously been convicted of any grade of theft;
3. A Class A misdemeanor if the value of the property stolen is $500 or more but less than $1,500;
4. A state jail felony if the value of the property stolen is $1,500 or more, but less than $20,000, or if the property consists of cattle, horses, sheep, swine, or goats, under the value of $20,000;
5. A felony of the third degree if the value of the property stolen is $20,000 or more but less than $100,000;

6. A felony of the second degree if the value of the property stolen is $100,000 or more but less than $200,000; or

7. A felony of the first degree if the value of the property stolen is $200,000 or more.

Theft of Trade Secrets

Often businesses, such as the Coca-Cola Company, have secret formulas, or like oil companies, have geophysical maps, which mean very much to those companies in their industries. They are known as trade secrets, and if someone without the consent of the owner makes a copy of a formula or of a map, he commits a felony of the third degree.

Theft of Service

A person commits theft of service if, with intent to avoid payment for service that he knows is provided only for compensation:

1. He intentionally or knowingly secures performance of the service by deception, or false token; or

2. Having control over disposition of services of another to which he is not entitled, he intentionally or knowingly diverts the other's services to his own use or benefit or to the benefit of another not entitled to them. An example is the often-complained-of practice by a county or city commissioner who uses the equipment and personnel of the county or city to build improvements on his private farm.

Intent to avoid payment is presumed if the actor absconds without paying for the service in circumstances where payment is ordinarily made immediately upon rendering of the service, as in hotels, motels, restaurants, and comparable establishments.

As with other theft offenses, the severity of the penalty increases with the value of the service stolen.

Bad Checks

The passing of bad checks (or "hot checks") is governed by two statutes. One makes it a Class C misdemeanor (unless it is for child support, in which case it is Class B) to pass a worthless check, regardless of the amount.

The other statute, entitled "Presumption of Theft by Check" requires that that actor obtained property or services by passing the check. The punishment is keyed to the theft statute and depends on the amount involved. One who has given a bad check for an existing debt cannot be prosecuted under this statute. Both statutes establish *prima facie* evidence of intent if the actor fails to make restitution within 10 days after receipt of notice by registered or certified mail.

Unauthorized Use of a Vehicle

A person commits a state jail felony if he intentionally or knowingly operates another's boat, airplane, or motor-propelled vehicle without the consent of the owner.

Aggregation of Amounts Involved in Theft

Formerly it was possible for a thief to commit a series of misdemeanor offenses in one single foray, yet he could be prosecuted only for each offense separately. Now if the offenses are part of one scheme or continuing course of conduct, they can be aggregated, or added together, resulting in prosecution for a felony offense.

Fraud

In fraud as in theft when amounts are obtained pursuant to one scheme or continuing course of conduct, whether from the same or several sources, the conduct may be considered as one offense and the amounts added together in determining the grade of offense. In actual practice, however, prosecution under this provision probably will be rare rather than frequent.

Fraud involves deception, and it takes on many forms of cheating and theft. By necessity the statutes dealing with fraud are technical and full of definitions too long and numerous to be presented in full in a book of this kind, but a fair discussion is given dealing with the more serious acts constituting the offense.

Forgery

"Forge" means:

1. To alter, make complete, execute, or authenticate any writing so that it purports:
   a. to be the act of another who did not authorize that act;
   b. to have been executed at a time or place or in a number sequence other than was in fact the case; or
   c. to be a copy of an original when no such original existed.
2. To issue, transfer, register the transfer of, pass, publish, or otherwise utter a writing that is forged within the meaning of paragraph 1 above.
3. To possess a writing that is forged with intent to use it to defraud.

"Writing" includes printing or any other method of recording information; it also includes money, coins, tokens, stamps, seals, credit cards, badges, and trademarks; and symbols of value, right, privilege, or identification.

Most forgeries, such as mentioned above, are Class A misdemeanors; but if the writing is or purports to be a will, codicil, deed, deed of trust, mortgage, security instrument, security agreement, credit card, check or similar sight order for payment of money, contract, release, or other commercial instrument, it is a state jail felony.

It is a felony of the third degree if the writing is or purports to be part of an issue of money, securities, postage or revenue stamps, or other instruments issued by state or national government or by a subdivision of either, or part of an issue of stock, bonds, or other instruments representing interests in or claims against another person.

Criminal Simulation

If, with intent to defraud, a person makes or alters an object, in whole or in part, so that it appears to have value because of age, antiquity, rarity, source, or authorship that it does not have; or he sells or passes an object so made or altered; or he possesses an object so made or altered, with intent to sell it or pass it; or he authenticates or certifies an object so made or altered as genuine or as different from what it is, he commits a Class A misdemeanor.

Credit Card Abuse

We are people accustomed to credit, and credit cards have come into such extensive use that public policy demands that their use be protected almost to the extent that our legal tender "money" is protected. The misuse of credit cards in the various forms it takes on is a state jail felony.

False Statement to Obtain Property or Credit

A person commits a Class A misdemeanor if he intentionally or knowingly makes a materially false or misleading written statement to obtain property or credit for himself or another. Credit in this case includes a loan of money, furnishing property or services on credit, extending the due date of an obligation, co-making, endorsing, or guaranteeing a note or other instrument for obtaining credit, a line or letter of credit, or a credit card.

Hindering Secured Creditors

A person who has signed a security agreement in property he/she is purchasing commits an offense if, with intent to hinder enforcement of the lien, he destroys, removes, conceals, encumbers, or otherwise harms or reduces the value of the property. The actor's guilty intent is presumed if he failed to make the payment when due, and, after demand, refused to deliver the property to the secured party. Penalties range from a Class C misdemeanor to a felony of the first degree, depending on the value of the property. Consumers who purchase goods on time can find themselves in trouble if they default on payments, then move and fail to notify the secured party of their new location.

Deceptive Business Practices

While the law provides penalties for numerous offenses against businesses, it also seeks to protect the consumer against offenses by businesses. A business or business firm, if it carries on a "deceptive sales contest," one in which it seeks to increase sales by offering prizes, or other instruments designed to enhance sales, commits a Class A misdemeanor. A sales contest honestly carried on is not forbidden; it is deception that is punished.

For example, a business may advertise that it will give away 1,000 prizes when in fact it gives only 500, or that the prizes will be of certain value when the value is less, or the business may rig the drawing of prizes so that only certain people closely related to the business will draw a prize.

Examples of other deceptive practices for which the same penalty is provided are: selling a mislabeled or adulterated product; using a scale or weight measure that shows a greater weight than the product sold actually has; advertising a product for sale as new or original when it is secondhand, altered, rebuilt, reconditioned, or reclaimed; advertising a product for sale with intent not to sell it as advertised, etc.

Commercial Bribery

The law binds a person in a position of trust to be faithful to his trust, and all of the following classes of persons are in positions of trust:

1. An agent or employee
2. A trustee, guardian, custodian, administrator, executor, conservator, receiver, or similar fiduciary
3. A lawyer, physician, accountant, appraiser, or other professional adviser
4. An officer, director, partner, manager, or other participant in the direction of the affairs of a corporation or association

A person in any such position of trust commits a state jail felony if he intentionally or knowingly solicits, accepts, or agrees to accept any benefit as consideration for violating a duty to a beneficiary or for otherwise causing harm to a beneficiary by act or omission. These are breaches of duty that involve a bribe, not the simple and small neglect of duty. The person who offers the benefit is also guilty of commercial bribery.

Rigging Publicly Exhibited Contest

A person commits a Class A misdemeanor if, with intent to affect the outcome (including the score) of a publicly exhibited contest, he offers, confers, or agrees to confer any benefit on, or threatens harm to:

1. A participant in the contest to induce him not to use his best efforts;
2. An official or other person associated with the contest; or
3. He tampers with a person, animal, or thing in a manner contrary to the rules of the contest.

The person who agrees to accept, or does accept, any benefit to affect the outcome of the contest or score also commits the offense.

Misapplication of Fiduciary Property or Property of Financial Institution

A person commits an offense if he intentionally, knowingly, or recklessly misapplies property (or money) he holds as a fiduciary (in trust) or property of a financial institution in a manner that involves substantial risk of loss to the owner of the property or to a person for whose benefit the property is held. The penalties for this offense vary according to the value of the property misapplied.

Securing Execution of Property by Deception

A person commits an offense if, with intent to defraud or harm any person, he, by deception, causes another to sign or execute any document affecting property or service or the pecuniary interest of any person. The penalty for the offense depends on the amount of property or money involved.

Fraudulent Destruction, Removal, or Concealment of Writing

A person commits a Class C misdemeanor if, with intent to defraud or harm another, he destroys, removes, conceals, alters, substitutes, or otherwise impairs the verity, legibility, or availability of a writing, other than a governmental record, and writing in this case includes:

1. Printing or any other method of recording information;
2. Money coins, tokens, stamps, seals, credit cards, badges, trademarks;
3. Symbols of value, right, privilege, or identification; and
4. Labels, price tags, or marking on goods

It is a state jail felony if the writing

1. Is a will or codicil of another, whether or not the maker is alive or dead and whether or not it has been admitted to probate; or
2. Is a deed, mortgage, deed of trust, security instrument, security agreement, or other writing for which the law provides public recording or filing, whether or not the writing has been acknowledged.

Offenses Against Public Administration

Bribery

A person commits a felony of the second degree if he intentionally or knowingly offers, confers, or agrees to confer on another, or solicits, accepts, or agrees to accept from another any benefit as consideration for the recipient's decision, vote, or exercise of discretion (including judicial) as a public servant, party official, or voter. The law excludes political contributions as defined by the election code, provided it is not given in consideration of some benefit. It is no defense that the benefit was not conferred until the decision was completed, or the public servant was out of office.

Coercion of Public Servant or Voter

A person commits a Class A misdemeanor if by coercion he

1. Influences or attempts to influence a public servant in a specific exercise of his official powers or a specific performance of his official duty; or
2. Influences or attempts to influence a voter not to vote or to vote in a particular manner. The offense is a felony of the third degree if the coercion involves a threat to commit a felony.

Improper Influence

A person commits a Class A misdemeanor if he privately addresses a representation, entreaty, argument, or other communication to any public servant who exercises or will exercise official discretion in an "adjudicatory proceeding" to influence the outcome of the proceeding on the basis of consideration other than those authorized by law. "Adjudicatory proceeding," as the term is here used, means any proceeding before a court or any other agency of the government in which the legal rights, powers, duties, or privileges of specified parties are determined.

It is highly improper, and now an offense mentioned above, if during the trial of a case a lawyer who is party to the suit approaches the judge or any member of the jury privately and tries to influence his decision in the case. A lawyer should shun the appearance of such conduct by avoiding any private meeting with the judge, except that specifically called for by the judge. If the judge calls for a private meeting with one of the attorneys in the case, he owes it to the opposing attorney to let him know the reason for the private conference. If he fails to do so, he probably leaves lingering in the mind of the opposing attorney some doubt as to the judge's fairness and impartiality.

Tampering with a Witness

One who gives or offers to a witness in an official proceeding anything of value to influence him to testify falsely, to withhold information, to elude a summons, or to absent himself from a legal proceeding to which he has been legally summoned commits a felony of the third degree.

A witness or prospective witness in an official proceeding who knowingly solicits, accepts, or agrees to accept any benefit with the understanding that it will influence him commits the same offense. It is a state jail felony.

Retaliation

A person commits a felony of the third degree if he intentionally or knowingly harms or threatens to harm another by an unlawful act in retaliation for or on account of the service of another as a public servant, witness, or informant.

Gift to Public Servant by Person Subject to his Jurisdiction

A public servant having regulatory or investigative authority or who exercises discretion in awarding public contracts commits a Class A misdemeanor if he solicits, accepts, or agrees to accept any benefit from one who will be affected by his decisions or investigations; and the person who will be affected commits an offense of the same degree if he offers, confers, or agrees to confer any benefit on a public servant that he knows the public servant is prohibited by law from accepting.

It is no offense, however, if the thing given is a fee required by law, or if the gift is trivial like a pencil or token of little or no value or a meal offered the public servant as a courtesy in ordinary fellowship or camaraderie, or a lawful contribution made under the election laws for the political campaign of an elective public servant.

Nepotism

A public official may not appoint, confirm the appointment of, or vote for the appointment or confirmation of the appointment of an individual to a position that is to be compensated from public funds if the person is related within the second degree by affinity or within the third degree by consanguinity to the person appointing or voting.

This statute is the basis of many opinions by the attorney general of the state. Some trouble arises because the law does not define degrees of kinship. It simply says, "related within the second degree of affinity or within the third degree by consanguinity," and it leaves officials, boards, and judges in doubt as to just what "degree" of kinship a first cousin, second cousin, or third cousin may be to the official.

Consanguinity means blood relation, and affinity means relation by marriage. The penalty for violation of the nepotism laws is a fine of not less than $100 nor more than $1,000.

Figures 6-1 and 6-2 will be helpful in determining degrees of kinship.

Violations of the Civil Rights of a Person in Custody

This significant new provision was passed by the Texas Legislature in 1979. It imposes criminal liability on any peace officer, jailer, or guard who, knowing his conduct is unlawful, intentionally denies or impedes a person in custody in the exercise or enjoyment of any right, privilege, or immunity. The offense is a Class A misdemeanor. The Texas Attorney General has concurrent jurisdiction with local authorities to investigate violations of this statute when there is death or serious bodily injury.

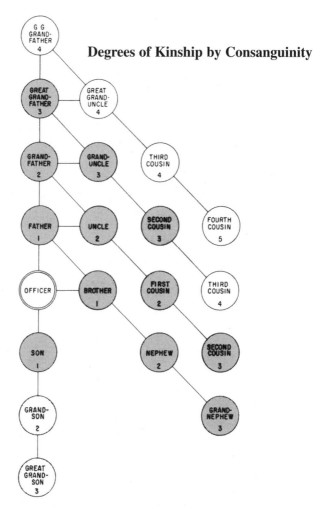

Degrees of Kinship by Consanguinity

Figure 6-1. An officer having authority to appoint persons to office could not appoint anyone related to him within the third degree by consanguinity. Female relatives may be substituted in the circles, as aunt for uncle, mother for father, etc. Shaded circles show those within the prohibited degrees of kinship. Numbers indicate the degrees of kinship.

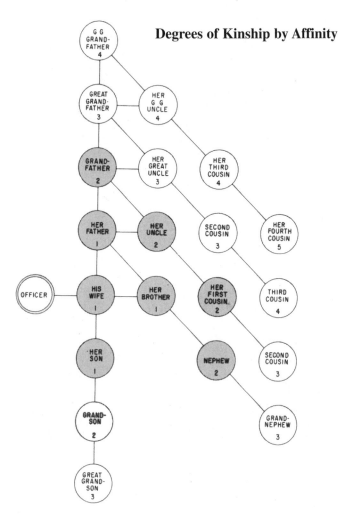

Degrees of Kinship by Affinity

Figure 6-2. An officer having authority to appoint persons to office could not appoint anyone related to him within the second degree by affinity. Shaded circles show those within the prohibited degrees of kinship. Numbers indicate the degrees of kinship. Female relatives may be substituted in the circles, as aunt for uncle, etc.

Official Oppression

A public servant acting under color of his office commits a Class A misdemeanor if he

1. Intentionally subjects another to mistreatment or to arrest, detention, search, seizure, dispossession, assessment, or lien that he knows is unlawful;
2. Intentionally denies or impedes another in the exercise or enjoyment of any right, privilege, power, or immunity, knowing that his conduct is unlawful; or
3. Intentionally subjects another to sexual harassment.

Misuse of Official Information

A public servant commits a misdemeanor if, in reliance on information to which he has access in his official capacity and which has not been made public, he

1. Acquires or aids another to acquire a pecuniary interest in any property, transaction, or enterprise that may be affected by the information;
2. Speculates or aids another to speculate on the basis of the information; or
3. As a public servant, coerces another into suppressing or failing to report information to a law enforcement agency.

Perjury and Other Falsification

Perjury

A person commits a Class A misdemeanor if, with intent to deceive and with knowledge of the statement's meaning:

1. He or she makes a false statement under oath or swears to the truth of a false statement previously made; and
2. The statement is required or authorized by law to be made under oath.

Aggravated Perjury

The offense above mentioned becomes aggravated perjury if it is made in connection with an official proceeding and is material. A statement is material, regardless of the admissibility of the statement under the rules of evidence, if it could have affected the course or outcome of the official proceeding.

If one making a false statement of the class of aggravated perjury retracts his false statement before completion of the testimony at the official proceeding, and before it becomes manifest that the falsity of the statement would be exposed, he commits no offense.

False Report to a Peace Officer

A person commits a Class B misdemeanor if, with intent to deceive, he knowingly makes a false statement to a peace officer conducting a criminal investigation and the statement is material to the investigation.

Tampering with or Fabricating Physical Evidence

A person commits a felony of the third degree if, while knowing that an investigation or official proceeding is pending or in progress, he:

1. Alters, destroys, or conceals any record, document, or thing with intent to impair its verity, legibility, or availability as evidence in the investigation or official proceeding; or

2. Makes, presents, or uses any record, document, or thing with knowledge of its falsity and with intent to affect the course or outcome of the investigation or official proceeding.

There is no offense under this provision if the record, document, or thing concealed is privileged or is the work product of the parties to the investigation. It was under similar federal law that the hassle over the Watergate tapes became so intense.

Tampering with Government Record

It is a Class A misdemeanor if a person knowingly makes a false entry in, or false alteration of, a governmental record; or makes, presents, or uses any record, document, or thing with knowledge of its falsity and with intent that it be taken as a genuine governmental record; or intentionally destroys, conceals, removes, or otherwise impairs the verity, legibility, or availability of a governmental record.

Impersonating a Public Servant

It is a Class A misdemeanor for a person to impersonate a public servant with intent to induce another to submit to his pretended official authority or to rely on his pretended official acts.

Obstructing Governmental Operation

Failure to Identify as a Witness

A person commits a Class C misdemeanor if he intentionally refuses to give his name, residence address, or date of birth to a peace officer who has lawfully arrested the person and requested the information. It is also an offense to give false or fictitious information.

Resisting Arrest or Search

If one intentionally prevents or obstructs a person he knows is a peace officer from effecting an arrest or search of the actor or another by using force against the peace officer, he commits a Class A misdemeanor. It is a felony of the third degree if the actor uses a deadly weapon to resist the arrest or search.

Evading Arrest

A person commits a Class B misdemeanor if he intentionally flees from a person he knows is a peace officer attempting lawfully to arrest him. It is a Class A misdemeanor if the actor uses a motor vehicle in flight.

Hindering Apprehension or Prosecution

A person commits an offense if, with intent to hinder the arrest, prosecution, conviction, or punishment of another for an offense, he

1. Harbors or conceals the other;
2. Provides or aids in providing the other with any means of avoiding arrest or effecting escape; or
3. Warns the other of impending discovery or apprehension.

This offense is a Class A misdemeanor. It is a defense against prosecution under (3) if the person giving the warning was in fact trying to bring the one warned into compliance with the law. This offense is a felony of the third degree if the person being aided has been charged with or convicted of a felony, and the actor is aware of this.

Escape

A person arrested for, charged with, or convicted of an offense commits an offense if he escapes from custody. This offense is a

Class A misdemeanor. An offense under this provision of the law, however, is a felony of the third degree if the actor

1. Is under arrest for, charged with, or convicted of a felony; or
2. Is confined in a secure correctional facility.

The offense becomes a felony of the first degree if the actor used or threatened to use a deadly weapon to effect his escape, or he causes serious bodily injury to another person.

An official or employee of an institution that is responsible for maintaining persons in custody commits an offense if he intentionally, knowingly, or recklessly permits or aids the escape of a person in custody. The offense is a Class A misdemeanor or a felony of the third degree depending on the kind of prisoner aided, whether he is charged with or convicted of a misdemeanor or felony, and whether he used a deadly weapon to escape.

Implements for Escape

It is a felony of the third degree to furnish an inmate in a penal institution a deadly weapon or anything else that may be useful for escape.

Bail Jumping and Failure to Appear

One who is released from custody with or without bond on condition that he subsequently appear commits an offense if he intentionally or knowingly fails to appear in accordance with the terms of his release. If the offense for which the person's appearance is required is punishable by fine only, then the offense is a Class C misdemeanor. If the offense for which the person's appearance is required is a felony then the person, by failing to appear, commits a felony of the third degree.

Barratry

The barratry statute was rewritten in the 1993 revised code. The penalty has been raised from a Class A misdemeanor to a felony of the third degree. It is an attempt to stop attorneys and their agents from engaging in the more blatant forms of chasing clients and cases. An attorney cannot solicit employment either in person or by telephone. He or she cannot pay prospective clients money or anything else of value to obtain legal representation. No communication can be mailed to the victim of an accident or disaster until the thirty-first day after the date on which the accident or disaster occurred.

Hindering Proceedings by Disorderly Conduct

A person commits a Class A misdemeanor if he intentionally hinders an official proceeding by noise or violent or tumultuous behavior or disturbance, or if he hinders such a proceeding and continues to do so after explicit official request to desist.

Voter Registration and Election Laws

Prior to 1966, a Texas voter was required to hold a poll tax receipt showing that he had paid his poll tax, or had to hold an exemption receipt showing that he was exempt from the tax. The poll tax law is no longer effective in Texas due to a ruling of the United States Supreme Court, but voters must register in order to vote.

Election officers are charged with the duty to discharge their obligations faithfully in conducting elections. Penalties are provided for their misconduct, ranging from cash fines to jail sentences to penitentiary sentences.

A person who knows he is disqualified to vote in an election and who votes anyway is guilty of a felony of the third degree.

One who procures, aids, or advises another to vote at an election, knowing the person is not qualified to vote, or procures, aids, or advises a person to vote more than once at the same election is guilty of a Class B misdemeanor.

Anyone who commits an illegal act while voting, such as showing his ballot to disclose his vote or giving the election judge a ballot other than the one the judge gave him at the polling place, can be fined.

There are numerous other penalties surrounding the election process. Those running for public office or involved in the election should become very familiar with these statutes.

Children—Compulsory School Attendance, Employment of Children, Contributing to Delinquency of a Child

After the Texas legislature decided that it was fair to tax a person who has no children, so that another's children can be educated, it had then to consider the question of whether that person had the right to keep his children out of school. The legislature decided that a person should be forced to send his children to school, if he was failing to do so. Thus, the compulsory school attendance law was enacted and this law carries punishment for the person who neglects to send his children to school.

Children are in a separate class from the adult with respect to employment. Any dangerous place or places where children may be exposed to immoral influences are "off limits" to them, and employers are held responsible when they expose children to such places through employment. It is not the law's intent that children should be forbidden to work; the intent is that when they work, they should be in places safe from physical danger and from moral danger.

Severe punishment is provided for adults who contribute to the delinquency of children. The following pages will show that the protection of children has had high priority with the legislatures of this state.

Compulsory School Attendance

It is the law in this state that parents shall send their children to school who are seven years of age through the academic year in which their 16th birthday occurred, and who are not high school graduates, for the entire school term in the district in which they reside or in the district where they may be transferred. Failure of a parent to do so is punishable by a fine of not less than $10 nor more than $50 for the first offense, not less than $20 nor more than $100 for the second offense, and not less than $50 nor more than $200 for subsequent offenses.

Of course, parents may send their children to a private or parochial school, instead of to the public schools. It is only required that children be sent to a suitable school, so their education may not be neglected.

Exceptions are:

1. Illness, or a state of health for which a reputable physician gives a certificate showing that school attendance is inadvisable and stating the period of time that such condition exists or may exist.
2. The parent is unable to compel the child to attend school. But then the child may be declared habitually truant, and face proceedings in juvenile court.

School Buses

School buses and other vehicles used as buses are required to be plainly marked on the front and on the rear in letters not less than six inches high with the words *School Bus*. When a vehicle transporting children stops, any other motor vehicle approaching it from any direction must be brought to a complete stop before proceeding in any direction. If the school bus vehicle is receiving or discharging passengers, then any other motor vehicle should not start or attempt to pass in any direction until the school bus vehicle has finished receiving and/or discharging passengers.

One who violates this provision is guilty of a misdemeanor, and if convicted can be fined or be confined in the county jail or both. If death results to any person, however, as a result of such a violation, the offender shall be punished as is now provided by law otherwise for the death of such person.

Employment of Children Under Fourteen

As a general rule, an employer commits a Class C misdemeanor if he employs a child under 14 years of age. The Texas Employment Commission may by rule authorize the employment of younger children as performers in theater, motion pictures, radio, or television.

It is illegal to hire a child who is 14 or 15 to work more than eight hours in one day or 48 hours in one week. If they are enrolled in school, it is also illegal to work them between 10 p.m. and 5 a.m. on a day followed by a school day, or between midnight and 5 a.m. on a day not followed by a school day. The commission can by rule determine when a hardship exists that would enable a child to work more hours.

The commission may by rule restrict the employment of children 14 years or older in hazardous occupations. The commission will declare an occupation hazardous if it has been so declared by an agency of the federal government, and the commission determines that it is particularly hazardous for the employment of children.

Offenses Against Public Order and Decency

Disorderly Conduct

A person commits an offense if he intentionally or knowingly

1. Uses abusive, indecent, profane, or vulgar language in a public place, and the language by its very utterance tends to incite an immediate breach of the peace;
2. Makes an offensive gesture or display in a public place, and the gesture or display tends to incite an immediate breach of the peace;
3. Creates, by chemical means, a noxious and unreasonable odor in a public place;
4. Abuses or threatens a person in a public place in an obviously offensive manner;
5. Makes unreasonable noise in a public place or in or near a private residence that he has no right to occupy;
6. Fights with another in a public place;
7. Enters on the property of another and for a lewd or unlawful purpose looks into a dwelling on the property through any window or other opening in the dwelling;
8. While on the premises of a hotel or similar establishment, for a lewd or unlawful purpose, looks into another guest room through a window or another opening in the room;
9. Discharges a firearm in a public place;
10. Displays a firearm or other deadly weapon in a public place in a manner calculated to alarm;
11. Discharges a firearm on or across a public road; or
12. Exposes his anus or genitals in a public place and is reckless about whether another may be present who will be offended or alarmed by his act.

These are all Class C misdemeanors, except for (9) and (10), which are Class B misdemeanors.

Obstructing a Highway or Other Passageway

A person commits a Class B misdemeanor if, without authority, he intentionally, knowingly or recklessly

1. Obstructs a highway, street, sidewalk, railway, waterway, elevator, aisle, hallway, entrance, or exit to which the public or a substantial group of the public has access, or any other place used for passage of persons, vehicles, or conveyances, regardless of the means of creating the obstruction and whether the obstruction arises from his acts alone or from his acts and the acts of others; or
2. Disobeys a reasonable request or order to move issued by a person the actor knows to be, or is informed is, a peace officer, a fireman, or a person with authority to control the use of the premises.

This provision, among other things, is intended to cover the takeover of buildings and passageways by protestors.

It is no offense if those assembled or obstructing move promptly when the order to move is given, or if they are assembled to hear a speech by an authorized speaker on economic, religious, or political questions in a peaceable manner.

Disrupting Meeting or Procession

A person commits a Class B misdemeanor if, with intent to prevent or disrupt a lawful meeting, procession, or gathering, he obstructs or interferes with the meeting, gathering, or procession by physical action or verbal utterance.

False Alarm or Report

A person commits a Class A misdemeanor if he knowingly initiates, communicates, circulates, or broadcasts a report of a present, past, or future bombing, fire, offense, or other emergency that he knows is false or baseless and that would ordinarily

1. Cause action by an official or volunteer agency organized to deal with emergencies;
2. Place a person in fear of imminent serious bodily injury; or
3. Prevent or interrupt the occupation of a building, room, place of assembly, place to which the public has access, or aircraft, automobile, or other mode of conveyance.

Harassment

A person commits a Class B misdemeanor if, with intent to harass, annoy, alarm, abuse, torment or embarrass, he

1. Communicates by telephone or in writing and makes an obscene comment or proposal;
2. Threatens in an alarming manner to inflict bodily injury or a felony against the person, her family or property;
3. Conveys a false report that another person has suffered death or serious bodily injury;
4. Makes repeated anonymous telephone calls that harass and annoy;
5. Makes a telephone call and intentionally fails to hang up; or
6. Knowingly permits a person to use his telephone to commit an offense under this section.

A person places a telephone call as soon as he dials a complete telephone number, whether or not a conversation ensues.

Stalking

It is a Class A misdemeanor for one to engage in a course of conduct directed at another person that the actor knows the other person will regard as threatening bodily injury or death for that person or a member of the person's family or household, or an offense against the person's property. The evidence must show that the person was in fact placed in fear of such injuries. A second offense is a third degree felony.

Abuse of Corpse

A person commits a Class C misdemeanor if, not authorized by law, he

1. Disinters, disturbs, removes, dissects, in whole or in part, carries away, or treats in a seriously offensive manner a human corpse;
2. Conceals a human corpse knowing it to be illegally disinterred;
3. Sells or buys a human corpse or in any way traffics in a human corpse; or
4. Transmits or conveys, or procures to be transmitted or conveyed, a human corpse outside the state.

Cruelty to Animals

A person commits a Class A misdemeanor if he intentionally or knowingly

1. Tortures or seriously overworks an animal;
2. Fails unreasonably to provide necessary food, care, or shelter for an animal in his custody;
3. Abandons unreasonably an animal in his custody;

4. Transports or confines an animal in a cruel manner;
5. Kills, injures, or administers poison to an animal belonging to another without legal authority or the owner's consent;
6. Causes one animal to fight with another; or
7. Uses a live animal as a lure in dog race training or in dog coursing on a racetrack.

It is an exception, however, if the person was or is engaged in bona fide experimentation for scientific research. It is a defense if the animal is killed or injured after being discovered on the actor's property attacking his livestock.

Shooting on a Public Road

A person commits a Class C misdemeanor if he intentionally or knowingly shoots or discharges any gun, pistol, or firearm on, along, or across a public road.

Promotion of Prostitution

A person commits a Class A misdemeanor if, acting other than as a prostitute receiving compensation for personally rendered prostitution services, he knowingly receives money or other property pursuant to an agreement to participate in the proceeds of prostitution. Prostitution itself is a Class B misdemeanor.

Compelling Prostitution

A person commits a felony of the second degree if he knowingly

1. Causes another by force, threat, or fraud to commit prostitution; or
2. Causes by any means a person younger than 17 years to commit prostitution.

Obscenity

The law forbidding obscenity is a classic example of the law trying to resolve conflicting values. On the one hand, we invariably feel a need to control that type of literature and film traditionally classified as "obscene." On the other hand, we place a high value on freedom of speech. It may be easy to place the label "obscene" on expressions or ideas of which we disapprove.

The United States Supreme Court has been grappling with this problem for years. The Texas statute is an attempt to comply with the court's rulings, yet express the will of the people.

The first task is to define the meaning of obscenity. Many older statutes were stricken because they were too vague. In Texas, "obscenity" is defined as material or a performance that:

(a) The average person applying contemporary community standards would find, taken as a whole, appeals to the pruient interest in sex;

(b) Depicts or describes:

    1. Patently offensive representations or descriptions of ultimate sex acts, normal or perverted, actual or simulated, including sexual intercourse, sodomy, or sexual bestiality; or

    2. Patently offensive representations or descriptions of masturbation, excretory functions, sadism, masochism, lewd exhibition of the genitals, the male or female genitals in a state of sexual stimulation or arousal, covered male genitals in a discernibly turgid state, or a device designed and marketed as useful primarily for stimulation of the human genital organs; and

(c) Taken as a whole, lacks serious literary, artistic, political, or scientific value

Certainly, no one can argue that this statute is vague. There are several offenses involving obscenity.

Obscene Display or Distribution

. It is a Class C misdemeanor for a person to intentionally or knowingly display or distribute an obscene photograph, drawing, or other obscene material and to be "reckless about whether a person is present who will be offended by the display."

Obscene Objects

The wholesale promotion of obscene material or devices is a felony of the third degree. The promotion of particular obscene material and devices, or obscene performances, is a Class A misdemeanor.

Sale, Distribution, or Display of Material Harmful to a Minor

"Harmful material" in this instance means "obscene material." A person commits a Class A misdemeanor if, knowing the material is harmful and the person is a minor, he (a) sells, distributes, exhibits, or possesses for sale, distribution, or exhibition to a minor harmful material; or (b) displays harmful material and is reckless about whether a minor is present who will be offended or alarmed by the display.

He commits a felony, however, of the third degree if one hires, employs, or uses a minor to do or accomplish or to assist in doing or accomplishing any of the acts mentioned in (a) and (b) above.

Sexual Performance by a Child

To fight the growing problem of child pornography, the Texas Legislature in 1977 added a provision making it a felony of the second degree to knowingly employ, authorize, or induce a child younger than 18 years of age to engage in a sexual performance. A sexual performance means any performance involving actual or simulated sexual intercourse, deviate sexual intercourse, sexual bestiality, masturbation, sadomasochistic abuse, or lewd exhibition of the genitals. A parent, legal guardian, or custodian of a child younger than 18 years, who consents to such performance, is also guilty of the offense and subject to the same penalty.

Offenses Against Public Health, Safety, and Morals

Driving While Intoxicated

Under the code, "intoxication" means not having the normal use of mental or physical faculties due to the ingestion of alcohol, drugs or a combination of the two, or having an alcohol concentration of 0.10 or more. As this is written, the legislature is considering a bill that would lower the legal level to 0.08.

Driving while intoxicated is one of the most common and tragic violations of law. It is a Class B misdemeanor to operate a motor vehicle in a public place while intoxicated. There is a minimum 72-hour confinement, unless the defendant had an open container of alcohol in his possession. Then the confinement is for six days.

It is a Class C misdemeanor for one to appear in a public place while intoxicated to the degree that she endangers herself or another. It is also a Class C misdemeanor to consume an alcoholic beverage while operating a motor vehicle in a public place if ". . . observed doing so by a peace officer."

Weapons

Many weapons are defined in the penal code and designated as unlawful, and they include the following: "club," which includes blackjack, nightstick, mace, and tomahawk, but is not limited to those named (it may include also a heavy wooden stick or iron bar or a combination of them); "explosive weapon"; "firearm";

"firearm silencer"; "handgun"; "illegal knife," which includes any knife capable of inflicting serious bodily injury or death, a throw-blade knife, dagger, bowie knife, sword, or spear; "knuckles"; "machine gun"; "short-barrel firearm," which means a rifle with a barrel length less than 16 inches or a shotgun with a barrel length less than 18 inches long.

Of course, one can own these things and display them as curios or antiques, but carrying them around in public places is unlawful.

Unlawfully Carrying Weapons

A person commits a Class A misdemeanor if he intentionally, knowingly, or recklessly carries on or about his person a handgun, illegal knife, or club. If he carries on or about his person and into any place lawfully licensed for the sale or service of alcoholic beverages any such weapon named, he commits a felony of the third degree.

It is an exception, however, and not an offense if the person carrying any such weapon is a peace officer in the actual discharges of his duties as a peace officer, or if he is a member of the armed forces or national guard or a guard employed by a penal institution. Neither is it an offense if the person is on his own premises or premises under his control, nor if he is traveling or engaging in lawful hunting or fishing or other lawful sporting activity. "Traveling" as used here means going on a journey—not just going downtown or to the corner grocery. "On or about his person" includes the passenger compartment of a person's automobile and pocket of his clothes.

It is now possible for ordinary citizens to apply for and obtain the right to carry a concealed handgun. Even so, there are restrictions on when and where the these license holders can carry their guns. The restrictions are as follows:

1. It is an offense to intentionally fail to conceal the gun.
2. It is an offense to carry a handgun on the premises
   a. Of a business authorized to sell alcoholic beverages;
   b. Where a high school, collegiate, or professional sporting event is taking place;
   c. Of a correctional facility;
   d. Of a hospital or nursing home;
   e. Of an amusement part;
   f. Of a church, synagogue, or place of religious worship; or
   g. Of any meeting of a governmental entity.
3. It is also an offense to carry a handgun while intoxicated.

These are all Class A misdemeanors, except for (a) and (c) above, which are felonies of the third degree.

Places Where Weapons are Prohibited

A person commits a third-degree felony if, with a firearm, he intentionally, knowingly, or recklessly goes

1. On the premises of a school or educational institution, whether public or private, without the permission or authorization of the institution;
2. On the premises of a polling place on the day of election;
3. In any government court or offices utilized by the court;
4. On the premises of a racetrack; or
5. Into a secured area of an airport.

Of course, it is an exception if he is a peace officer in the actual discharge of his duties.

Unlawful Possession of a Firearm by a Felon

A person who has been convicted of a felony involving an act of violence or threatened violence to a person or property commits a felony of the third degree if, before the fifth anniversary of the person's release from confinement, he possesses a firearm away from the premises where he lives. This provision even forbids him to hunt game with a gun away from where he lives. There probably will be some amendment of this feature of the law.

Prohibited Weapons

A person commits an offense if he intentionally or knowingly possesses, manufactures, transports, repairs, or sells

1. An explosive weapon;
2. A machine gun;
3. A short-barrel firearm;
4. A firearm silencer;
5. A switchblade knife;
6. Knuckles;
7. Armor-piercing ammunition;
8. A chemical dispensing device; or
9. A zip gun.

An offense involving these weapons is a felony of the third degree, except for numbers 5 and 6, which are Class A misdemeanors.

Unlawful Transfer of a Firearm

A person commits a Class A misdemeanor if he

1. Sells, rents, leases, loans, or gives a handgun to any person knowing that the person to whom the handgun is to be delivered intends to use it unlawfully or in the commission of an unlawful act;
2. Intentionally sells, rents, leases, or gives or offers to sell, rent, lease, or give to any child younger than 18 years any firearm; or

3. Intentionally, knowingly, or recklessly sells a firearm or ammunition for a firearm to any person who is intoxicated.

It is an exception in (2) above if the child is accompanied by his parent or guardian or the person who has custody of him or has written permission from the one in parental position.

Interstate Purchase

A resident of this state may, if not otherwise precluded by law, purchase firearms, ammunition, reloading components, or firearms accessories in contiguous states. Except for this provision, federal law would prevent Texans from purchasing firearms in neighboring states.

Gambling

A person commits a Class C misdemeanor if he

1. Makes a bet on the partial or final result of a game or contest or on the performance of a participant in a game or contest;
2. Makes a bet on the result of any political nomination, appointment, or election or on the degree of success of any nominee, appointee or candidate; or
3. Plays and bets for money or other things of value at any game played with cards, dice, or balls.

It is a defense to prosecution under this provision that

1. The actor engaged in gambling in a private place;
2. No person received any economic benefit other than personal winnings; and
3. Except for the advantage of skill or luck, the risk of losing and the chances of winning were the same for all participants.

Thus if gambling is done in a private home as a social affair no offense is committed, unless there is something rigged or unfair giving an advantage to one or more that is not available to others. It is also a defense if the actor reasonably believes his conduct was permitted under the Bingo Enabling Act, the Charitable Raffle Enabling Act, the Texas Racing Act, or the State Lottery Act.

Gambling Promotion

A person commits a Class A misdemeanor if he intentionally or knowingly does one of the following acts:

1. Operates or participates in the earnings of a gambling place;
2. Receives, records, or forwards a bet or offer to bet;
3. For gain, becomes a custodian of anything of value bet or offered to be bet;
4. Sells chances on any game or contest or political appointment or contest; or
5. Sets up or promotes a lottery.

Keeping a Gambling Place

A person commits a Class A misdemeanor if he knowingly uses or permits another to use as a gambling place any real estate, building, room, tent, vehicle, boat, or other property whatsoever owned by him or under his control, or rents or lets any such property with a view of expectation that it be so used.

Communicating Gambling Information

A person commits a Class A misdemeanor if he, with intent to further gambling, knowingly communicates information as to bets, betting odds, or changes in betting odds, or he knowingly provides, installs, or maintains equipment for the transmission or receipt of such information.

Possession of Gambling Device or Equipment

A person commits a Class A misdemeanor if he knowingly owns, manufactures, transfers, or possesses any gambling device that he knows is designed for gambling purposes or any equipment that he knows is designed as a subassembly or essential part of a gambling device. The offense is the same if the device or part thereof is an altered device or part.

Testimonial Immunity

A party to a gambling offense may be required to furnish evidence or testify about the offense, but in this case he is exempt from prosecution for the offense. This is a design of the law to obtain evidence that may otherwise be impossible to obtain, and it is based upon the premise or theory that it is better to catch some of the offenders, especially the leaders, even if one or more of the other offenders have to go free of punishment.

Conclusion

Even though this has been a complex chapter, we have only skimmed the surface of Texas criminal law. There are many provisions that have not been covered, such as the recent statute prohibiting "Organized Crime." Citizens having a problem or questions concerning specific criminal statutes should seek the advice of a competent attorney, because specific situations may modify what appears to be a simple textbook answer to a problem.

7. Regulatory Agencies

Administrative law is today the most rapidly growing branch of the American legal system. Texas alone has more than 118 such agencies. An administrative agency is a governmental body with responsibility for implementing a particular piece of legislation. These agencies are usually a microcosm of the three branches of government: they have rule-making power (legislative), enforcement power (executive), and the power to hold hearings and make decisions (judicial). At all levels, there is increasing reliance on administrative agencies to carry out the business of government.

Some agencies (such as the State Board of Education) are mandated by the Texas Constitution. Most, however, are created by the legislature. These agencies have only those powers expressly conferred on them by their enabling legislation. In most cases, their procedures are controlled by the Texas Administrative Procedure Act. In addition, under the Texas Sunset Law, state agencies must periodically come before the legislature to justify their existence and be legislatively renewed. Otherwise, they are automatically abolished.

To look at all these agencies and their roles would be a book in itself. Accordingly, we will look at only a couple of agencies that have significant impact on ordinary citizens. Current regulations and rulings of all Texas agencies are published in the *Texas Register,* which can be found in many public libraries.

Regulatory Agencies for Labor and Traffic

The Texas Workforce Commission

The responsibilities of the old Texas Employment Commission and other agencies have been consolidated into the Texas Workforce Commission. Its purpose is to operate "an integrated workforce development system." It administers the unemployment compensation program and provides job training and employment-related educational programs. It also administers the laws regulating labor.

Eight-Hour Work Day

Eight hours, with few exceptions, constitutes a legal day's work, and it applies to laborers working on construction for the state as well as for private industry.

Employment of Children

For most purposes, it is against the law to employ children under 14 years of age. A child who is 14 or 15 cannot be employed to work more than eight hours in one day, or 48 hours in one week. A person, 14 or 15, who is enrolled in school, is forbidden to work between the hours of midnight and 5 a.m. on any day, and between the hours of 10 p.m. and 5 a.m. on a day followed by a school day. This law is administered by the Texas Workforce Commission.

Discrimination and Blacklisting

Any corporation, or receiver, or any agent or officer of a corporation who discriminates against anyone seeking employment because of his having participated in a strike is subject to criminal penalties.

One is guilty of "blacklisting" if he places the name of any former employee on any list or in any book, or publishes it in a newspaper, periodical, or letter intending to prevent him from securing employment with any other employer, or prospective employer. This is punishable by a fine of not less than $50 nor more than $250, or imprisonment in jail for not less than 30 nor more than 90 days.

It is not an offense, however, for the former employer to give, upon the request of the discharged employee or prospective employer, a true statement giving the reasons for the discharge, and the statement cannot be used against the former employer as a cause for an action for libel, either civil or criminal.

Servants or Employees Not to be Coerced

No person, firm, or corporation, nor the representatives of any employer may lawfully coerce or require any servant or employee to deal with or purchase any article of food or clothing, or merchandise of any kind whatever from any person, corporation, association, or company or at any place or store. No employee may be excluded from work or be blacklisted for failure to deal with any person or any firm, company, or corporation, or for failure to purchase any item of food, clothing, or other merchandise. A violation of this provision carries a criminal penalty.

Interfering with Labor or Vocation or Lawful Picketing

It is an offense for anyone to prevent, or attempt to prevent, by the use of force or violence, or the threat of the use of force or violence, any person from engaging in any lawful vocation within the state or from engaging in peaceful and lawful picketing.

Highway Traffic Safety Measures

Automobile and truck travel on the highways has reached such a volume that it poses a special danger problem for the operators of those motor vehicles and others, and much property damage results from it. For this reason, the legislature has enacted comprehensive and extensive laws to reduce the danger and has set up a Department of Public Safety and a highway patrol system. Drivers of motor vehicles on the highways must qualify for and have in their immediate possession driver's licenses, and the vehicles themselves must be registered and licensed and must be certified annually to be in safe mechanical condition for travel on the highways.

The License to Drive

Five kinds of licenses for driving on the highways are issued by the department: Classes A, B, C and M.

1. The Class C license is the one commonly issued to drivers of automobiles and pickup trucks and panel trucks of carrying capacity up to 2,600 pounds. A person 18 years of age or older who has passed successfully the driver's test given by the department may be issued a Class C license. A person 16 years of age or older may be issued a Class C license if he has completed successfully a driver's training course approved by the department and has passed successfully the driver's test given by the department. A person at least 16 years of age may be issued a permit to drive if:
   (a) The person has successfully completed the classroom phase of an approved driver education course and has successfully passed all phases of the driver test by the department; or

(b) The person has successfully passed the department's driving test, and it appears to the department that refusal to issue a license to the applicant would work an unusual economic hardship upon the family of the applicant, or it appears that the license should be issued to the applicant on account of sickness or illness of members of the applicant's family, or that failure to issue the license to the applicant would be detrimental to the applicant or to his or her family.

2. A Class B driver's license permits a person to drive a single vehicle with a gross weight exceeding 2,600 pounds, or a vehicle with a gross vehicle weight rating of 26,000 pounds or more, towing a vehicle other than a farm trailer, with a weight not more than 10,000 pounds, or a farm trailer that does not exceed 20,000 pounds or a bus and any vehicle authorized under a Class C license. To obtain this license one must be at least 18 years of age.

3. A Class A driver's license permits a person to drive any vehicle or combination of vehicles, including all vehicles authorized under Class B or C, with the exception of motorcycles or mopeds.

4. A Class M driver's license permits a person to drive a motorcycle or moped. One must hold this license to drive one of these vehicles; the other regular licenses do not cover them.

No driver's license of any type may be issued to a person under 15 years of age.

The Requirement of Insurance

It is illegal to operate a motor vehicle in Texas without complying with the Texas Motor Vehicle Safety Responsibility Act. Compliance requires that a driver have either a qualified liability insurance policy, or a surety bond, or a cash bond in the amount of $55,000 on deposit with the state comptroller or the county judge where the vehicle is registered. A person may be self-insured if he or she has more than 25 motor vehicles in his or her name. He or she must, however, have a certificate of self insurance issued by the Department of Public Safety. The department will issue this certificate if satisfied the person is able to comply with any judgments against them.

The law further requires drivers to furnish to any law enforcement officer on request ". . . information concerning evidence of financial responsibility . . ." The failure to "give information" raises a rebuttable presumption of failure to maintain financial responsibility. In most cases, this information will be evidence of an insurance policy.

Traffic Laws—Rules of the Road

The Department of Public Safety publishes and distributes for the use of applicants for drivers' licenses a pamphlet containing the information a person must know before he can be licensed to drive on the highways, and it is recommended that all prospective applicants obtain and study this pamphlet before going for the examination. It is not considered necessary to include that information here.

Since we are all subject to accidents, however, and we dread their consequences, it seems well to comment on what to do when an accident occurs, because accidents that cause considerable property damage, personal injury, or death bring on tensions and excitement, and in their excitement, people sometimes do things or neglect to do things which they regret.

Accidents Involving Personal Injury

When anyone is in an accident involving personal injury or death, if he is unhurt, he is required by law to stop and give aid.

Neglect to give his aid under such circumstances is a criminal offense. He is obligated to ask what injuries were suffered and to offer assistance. If requested to do so and his vehicle is capable of being driven, he should take the injured person or persons to a doctor or hospital for treatment. If his vehicle cannot be driven, he should make an effort to find others to take the injured for treatment.

Statements Made at the Scene of the Accident

It is a rule of evidence that statements made by anyone involved in an accident, immediately after the accident or at the scene of the accident, can be given in evidence by those who hear the statements. Consequently these may be damaging to a person in court if a lawsuit or criminal action is brought against him because of the accident. So often in the excitement immediately following an accident, a person misjudges the facts or the cause of the accident, and he may misjudge them wholly to his detriment.

A person involved in an accident may feel the urge to immediately confess that it is all his fault, especially if there is personal injury involved or considerable property damage. It is wise, however, to refrain from making any statements that would be totally against his interest. He needs to take time to examine as many aspects of the accident as possible. This is not to say he should be rude or bellicose toward the other parties involved. He can be sympathetic and say he is sorry that the accident occurred and otherwise show concern for anyone injured or whose vehicle has been damaged without making statements against his own interest.

The person involved in the accident may find that there are circumstances in his favor. In fact, he may find that all of the circumstances are in his favor. If this is the case, he owes it to his insurer not to make statements that will cost money unnecessarily, and he owes it to himself not to make his defense more difficult than is necessary.

In most instances, traffic officers will arrive on the scene, for they are supposed to be called to the scene either by someone involved in the accident or by some other person. Of course, it is the duty of the officers to make a careful investigation and to take notes so that their testimony of the facts can be used if they are requested by the proper authority.

Generally, an officer will question the parties involved and report the answers in a written statement. Usually, the officer will ask the person questioned if he would care to sign this statement. Of course, if the statement is altogether favorable, one might be glad to sign it, but if the statement is partially or wholly unfavorable to him, it is best that he decline signing it. It is proper for a person to state that though he is fully covered by insurance and expects his insurer to cover any liability he may have in the matter, he would prefer to obtain his insurer's approval before making any statement and for that reason would decline to sign it.

Let us suppose that this accident appears only to involve some damage to the other person's car and that its occupant gave, and signed, a statement saying that he suffered no personal injury. In this case, if the person who appears to be responsible for the accident has an urge to be decent and honorable about it, he may honestly feel it his duty to sign that statement naming him as the party in the wrong. Before he signs this, he should remember that in doing so, he is placing the total liability on his insurer.

Once he reports the accident to his insurer, the adjuster will go to settle the claim for damages, whatever they may be. The adjuster, however, may now find that the opposite party has obtained a zealous lawyer anxious to make a fee and who has convinced his client that he has sustained a bad back injury; an injury serious enough that it should not be settled for less than a few thousand dollars. For this reason, it is just generally good judgment not to sign any statements that are clearly against one's own interests.

8. Justice and the Code of Criminal Procedure

The Texas Penal Code defines criminal offenses and prescribes the punishment for them. The Code of Criminal Procedure describes how the criminal laws are to be administered, and, as will presently be seen, it gives guarantees to all people within the borders of this state against oppression and wrongful punishment. The theory of the law is that it is better to let the guilty go unpunished than it is to punish the innocent. It is unfortunate that the guilty often find easy escape under these provisions.

Our present Code of Criminal Procedure became effective on January 1, 1966. The objects of the code are declared as "to embrace rules applicable to the prevention and prosecution of offenses against the laws of this state, and to make the rules of procedure in respect to the prevention and punishment of offenses intelligible to the officers who are to act under them, and to all persons whose rights are to be affected by them." It seeks:

1. To adopt measures for preventing the commission of crime;
2. To exclude the offender from all hope of escape;
3. To ensure a trial with as little delay as is consistent with the ends of justice;
4. To bring to the investigation of each offense on the trial all the evidence tending to produce conviction or acquittal;

5. To ensure a fair and impartial trial; and
6. The certain execution of the sentence of the law when declared.

The Texas Code of Criminal Procedure and the Texas Constitution provide protections to citizens that are consistent with those provided by the United States Constitution. The United States Supreme Court has ruled, in a whole line of cases, the rights enumerated in the Bill of Rights are applicable to the states, essentially by means of the Fourteenth Amendment.

Due Course of Law

The Fourteenth Amendment asserts that no one shall be deprived of "life, liberty, or property" without "due process of law." The Texas Constitution has a similar provision. It states that no citizen shall be deprived of "life, liberty, property, privileges, or immunities . . . except by the due course of the laws of the land." The courts have held that "due process of law" and "due course of law" are equivalent terms. These provisions protect us and our property against arbitrary and unfair actions by government.

Rights of Accused

In all criminal prosecutions the accused is entitled to have a speedy public trial by an impartial jury. He has the right to demand the nature and cause of the accusation against him, and to be presented with a copy of the charges. He is not compelled to give evidence against himself, and he has the right to defend himself through testimony, through counsel, or both. He must be confronted by the witnesses against him and can exercise compulsory process of law to obtain witnesses in his favor. No person must answer for a felony unless he is indicted by a grand jury.

Right to Counsel

A defendant in an adversarial criminal case is entitled to be represented by an attorney. If it is a proceeding that could result in confinement, and the defendant is "indigent," he is entitled to a court-appointed attorney. For purposes of this provision, indigent is defined as "a person who is not financially able to employ counsel." A defendant may, however, "voluntarily and intelligently" in writing waive (or surrender) his right to counsel.

Searches and Seizures

The law provides that people are safe from all unreasonable seizures and searches of their persons, houses, papers, and possessions. No warrant to search any place or to seize any person or thing can be issued without describing it as nearly as possible, nor without probable cause supported by an oath or an affirmation.

Right to Bail

All prisoners are bailable unless for capital offenses when the proof is evident. This provision must not be construed as to prevent bail after indictment found upon examination of the evidence, in such a manner as prescribed by law. Bail is the security given by the accused that he will appear and answer before the proper court. It is not a punishment for the accused.

Habeas Corpus

The Texas Constitution provides that the writ of *habeas corpus* shall never be suspended. This writ means "let's have the body," and is used when some person is being deprived of his liberty, to challenge the reasons for his being held. It is an order directing the officer or other person holding the individual to produce him bodily before the court to justify the custody. This is the means used by many persons to challenge the constitutionality of their convictions long after the time for appeal has passed. It is used in child custody cases when one party has custody in violation of a court order.

Cruelty Forbidden

In language almost identical to the Eighth Amendment of the U.S. Constitution, the Texas Constitution forbids excessive bail, excessive fines, and the infliction of cruel and unusual punishment.

Double Jeopardy

The Constitution states that no person shall be twice put in jeopardy for life or liberty for the same offense. This is to prevent the government from harassing certain individuals by subjecting them to repeated prosecutions for the same offense. The defendant may have been "put in jeopardy" in a case even though it never reached a final verdict.

Once a jury is impaneled and witnesses sworn, jeopardy "attaches" and the defendant cannot be retried for the same offense. This rule does not apply if the proceeding is brought to a close prematurely at the request of the defendant. Nor does it apply to the various emergency situations that can cause a court to terminate a proceeding, such as sickness of jury or the judge, or a hung jury.

Right to Trial by Jury

Every person accused of a criminal offense is guaranteed the right of trial by jury. The accused cannot waive the right of trial by jury if he is charged with a capital felony, one that is punishable by death. If the offense is one that does not carry the death penalty he can waive this right, but only with the court's consent and the consent of the attorney representing the state, both made in writing and entered in the case record.

The accused cannot waive the right to a jury trial if he is not represented in court by an attorney. If he has no attorney representing him and he wishes to waive the right of trial by a jury, the court must first appoint an attorney to represent him. If the state intends to demand the death penalty, written notice of its intention must be filed with the court at least 15 days before the trial date. When the notice is given, the defendant cannot waive the right of trial by jury, and the trial cannot be held until the expiration of the 15-day period. One can see that the law seeks to protect the accused even against himself.

Freedom of Speech and of the Press

Like the federal Constitution, the state constitution provides that "no law shall ever be passed curtailing the liberty of speech or of the press." This, of course, is one of the bedrocks of a free society. This is why a court will never enjoin a newspaper or magazine from printing a false, libelous story. As the Texas Supreme Court has said: "Punishment for the abuse of the right, not prevention of its exercise, is what the provision contemplates."

Religious Belief

No person shall be disqualified to give evidence in any court of this state on account of his religious belief; but all oaths or affirmations shall be administered in the mode most binding upon the conscience, and shall be taken subject to the pains and penalties of perjury.

Many people feel that it is wrong to swear, even to the truth of statements made in court; and for this reason the courts will, to these persons, administer affirmations instead of oaths. One who affirms falsely is punishable the same as if he had sworn falsely.

Outlawry and Transportation

No citizen shall be outlawed, nor shall any person be transported out of the state for any offense committed within the same.

In many foreign countries people may be expatriated or banished from their country; often this is the punishment for a losing politician.

Corruption of Blood

No conviction shall work corruption of blood or forfeiture of estate.

A person may be convicted of a heinous crime, but he cannot be deprived of his property because of it. He can inherit property and can be inherited from, the same as if he had committed no crime.

Forfeiture of Contraband

In spite of the above provision, the state may seize property used or intended to be used in the commission of certain felonies, including the proceeds from those felonies. This property is called "contraband." The attorney for the state, however, must begin civil forfeiture proceedings within 30 days after the seizure.

In this proceeding, the owner of the property has the burden of proving that he or she owned the property before the date of the offense, and did not consent to the use of the property in the commission of a felony. This is the "innocent owner defense." It is not necessarily a defense that all criminal charges have been dropped or dismissed. Forfeiture procedures have stirred much national controversy. They have been the source of substantial financial support for local law enforcement. Many state statutes continue to face challenges as to their constitutionality. So far, the Texas statute has been upheld by the courts.

Defendant Confronted by Witnesses

A defendant has a right to be confronted by the witnesses against him, except in certain situations where deposition testimony will be heard. This provision prevents a person from being convicted by innuendo and rumor. It may occasionally allow the guilty to go free, when the witnesses against them are frightened and too intimidated to come into open court and testify.

What To Do When Accused of Crime

An individual accused of a felony is, with a few exceptions, arrested and taken into custody by some law officer, the sheriff or his deputy, a constable, a policeman, a United States Marshal, a member of the Federal Bureau of Investigation, or some other officer, and he is generally locked up in some jail. The law requires that there be probable cause for an arrest. The fact that one is arrested and locked in jail, however, does not prove he is guilty. It does mean, with few exceptions, that there is probable cause for his being taken into custody.

There is still much to do before a person is pronounced guilty. Under our system of law, one is presumed to be innocent until he has been *proven guilty beyond a reasonable doubt.* The burden of proof of guilt rests on the government under whose authority the person is accused of and held for a crime. The proof of guilt must be so convincing that there is no reasonable doubt to the contrary. If the proof falls short of this test, the accused must be set free because probable guilt or any other halfway measures in criminal law are not acceptable.

It is true that there are different sentences or degrees of punishment, but the proof of guilt beyond a reasonable doubt is still required before any degree of punishment can be inflicted upon the accused.

So it is that anyone arrested is still a long way from being convicted of the crime for which he is accused, and our criminal laws, the rules of criminal procedure, the Texas Constitution, and the United States Constitution afford the accused a very wide latitude in defending himself. In this respect, his advantages are greater in state courts than in federal courts. Judges in state courts are not allowed as much discretion of comment as judges in federal courts, and they are just generally more lenient as to the limits a lawyer can go in the interest of his client.

Often a person accused of a revolting crime goes free even though the public expresses disgust at the outcome of the trial; there are some miscarriages of justice. No thinking person, however, could wish to return to that system of trial under which Jesus of Nazareth was handed over to be punished, indeed crucified, because of the shouts of the people even after he had been found innocent.

Anyone accused of a crime should take steps in his own defense. The law provides him the means, but he must exercise them. The first thing he should do after being arrested is to hire a competent lawyer, and this should be done before he makes any statement to the arresting officer, to the press, or to others who may question him.

A good answer to all questions would be, "Let me have my lawyer present, and then I shall answer whatever questions he approves." In this way, a lawyer does not have to spend so much of his efforts in trying to overcome the adverse effects of statements made before he gets the case. Often, the accused makes a statement before talking to his lawyer and later repudiates it claiming that he made it under duress.

It is indeed difficult, and often impossible, for a lawyer to overcome the adverse effects of confessions by the accused. No one has to make a statement to the arresting officers or to investigators before or after he is put in jail or even in the courtroom. It is basic in our law that no one can be forced to testify against himself.

Therefore, anyone accused should let his lawyer determine which, if any, questions he should answer. Since this is a basic right, there is no wrong in holding doggedly to it. There may, in fact, be some advantage in making a statement, but the accused is in no position to judge this advantage, if it does exist.

The defense lawyer must be the architect and builder of the defense, and the more serious the charge, the stronger the foundation must be, since the prosecutor will try his best to put the accused in a bad light. The accused needs an advocate to put him in as favorable a light as possible.

Indeed, it is midway between these positions that the jury will try to find the truth. This is not to say that any false representations should be made, but by these opposing efforts both sides of the question of "guilt" or "innocence" are brought before the court, and each side will try to do its best. Whatever the prosecutor brings before the jury will be designed to condemn the accused; whatever the defense attorney brings will be designed to exonerate him.

The accused must bear in mind that the arresting officers and the investigators, when trying to get answers to their questions and asking him to sign a statement, are by circumstance on the side of those who seek to convict; and the accused will serve himself well by saying nothing without benefit of legal counsel.

Suppose, however, the accused person is in no financial position to hire a lawyer, or he might be in an area where not even one person knows him and finds himself destitute as far as help from friends is concerned. If he qualifies as "indigent," as stated above, the judge is required to appoint him a lawyer. In some jurisdictions he can be represented by the public defender. If the defendant is able to make bond, however, some judges will conclude that he is not indigent and can afford to hire his own lawyer.

Once the accused has hired a lawyer, or one has been appointed for him, he should then very carefully follow his lawyer's suggestions and instructions. His lawyer will have him brought into a conference room, out of the earshot of others, and it is at this first conference that he must win his lawyer by telling him the truth. He should tell the whole true story, even though he may be embarrassed and ashamed to do so.

The lawyer is entitled to have straight answers and it is absolutely necessary, for he can never put his heart into the case until he is sure that he has the whole truth. He must know everything that the accused knows so he can prepare for the onslaughts that will be made upon his client in the courtroom.

The accused should bear in mind also, in a case where a lawyer has been provided for him by the court, that the lawyer, even though he is bound by his profession and the appointment to represent the accused regardless of pay, will have a better feeling toward the accused if there is some sincere promise of compensation for his services.

The appointed lawyer, of course, cannot demand it, but the accused should avoid, as far as possible, the risk of making his lawyer feel that he is wasting his time and talents. He should not be too impatient, for the nature of the case may hinder the lawyer from doing all of the things the accused wants him to do. For example, the nature of the offense may make it impossible for the lawyer to provide bail so that the accused could be free pending trial date, or it may be that the accused is such a poor risk that the lawyer could not afford to furnish bail.

Once the lawyer has conferred with the accused, however, and has been given the whole truth and he has accepted employment or has accepted appointment by the judge, he can, and will, go to work with all his skill to "bring his client clear." It may be that the crime is so bad that it is revolting to think of it, but making out a case against the accused is left to the district attorney. It is the business of this lawyer to defend the case, and he will consider it as a matter of personal pride if he can escort his client out of the courtroom a free man.

If it happened that he knew his client was guilty, would he have conscientious scruples and remorse at seeing him go free because of his skill in handling the case? He would not, because his commitment to his client was to do the best he could for him, and because the judge trying the case expected no less of him as attorney for the defense—while at the same time expecting the prosecuting attorney to do his best for a conviction. Also, the high calling of his honorable profession demands that he do his best for his client, and our system of justice assumes that a lawyer will, and must, carry his point if he can.

Plea Bargaining

In our system, major criminal trials get a great deal of attention. In fact, only a small percentage of criminal cases ever go to trial. Most are resolved by the process known as plea bargaining. This occurs when the prosecuting attorney and defense attorney reach agreement on the plea to be made by the defendant and the penalty he will receive.

For years, this process was surreptitious and somewhat hypocritical. Now it is open and above-board. It is also the subject of considerable criticism. It is argued that it allows career criminals to "cop a plea" for a much lower penalty than a jury would give them. On the other hand, it may pressure an innocent defendant into a guilty plea to avoid the risk of conviction and a more onerous penalty.

The Mode of Trial in a Criminal Case

Here briefly is the procedure followed in a criminal case, a felony case, in which the accused may be given a penitentiary sentence.

Trial in the District Court

The trial will be before a jury, and a list of the venirement must be given to the defendant two full days (48 hours) before the trial begins. When the state and the defendant have announced they are ready for trial, or if they do not announce ready and the motions for postponement have been overruled, the names of those summoned as jurors will be called.

A fine of $50 may be assessed against any juror summoned and not present, and an attachment may be issued by request of either the defendant or the state for an absent summoned juror to be brought immediately before the court.

To those veniremen present in the court, the judge will have this oath administered:

> You, and each of you, solemnly swear that you will make true answers to such questions as may be propounded to you by the court, or under its directions, touching on your service and qualifications as a juror, so help you God.

The judge will then hear excuses from those who desire to be excused from jury duty, and he may excuse anyone whose reason he considers valid. By consent of both parties, anyone on the venire may be excused, but the judge does not always grant a request to be excused.

Either party may challenge the array, which is the whole panel of prospective jurors, but only on the ground that the officer summoning them willfully did so to secure a conviction or acquittal. It is not often that such a challenge is sustained because it is not often that those grounds exist; but the challenge is available to the party who feels it should be used. If the challenge is sustained, all of the array of prospective jurors will be discharged.

Then a new venire is summoned, and a list of their names is given to the defendant as in the first instance. After the new group has taken the oath, or in case of the original group, if no challenge to the array has been made, or if made has been overruled by the court, the prospective jurors will be tested by the following questions by the court or under his directions:

1. Except for voter registration, are you a qualified voter in this county and state, under the constitution and laws of this state?
2. Have you ever been convicted of theft or any felony?
3. Are you under indictment or legal accusation for theft or any felony?

A prospective juror who gives a "yes" answer to questions nos. 1 and 2 and a "no" answer to no. 3 will be qualified, unless subsequent questioning shows he is not. Each side, however, first the state and then the defense, will try diligently, by asking questions, to ascertain whether there is still cause for challenging a venireman, and if the attorney for either side finds cause for challenging, he will do so. The judge will immediately rule on the challenge by sustaining it or overruling it. If the challenge is sustained, the venireman is excused; and if the challenge is overruled, the venireman is not yet disqualified.

Each side, though, has 15 peremptory challenges if it is a case where the death penalty may be given, and 10 in a felony case where the death penalty is not asked for by the state. The attorney who sought to disqualify the venireman for cause can still keep him off the jury by using one of these peremptory challenges against him. In this instance, he excuses the venireman without having to give any reason.

The reason must not be based on race, however. In *Batson v. Kentucky* (1988), the United States Supreme Court ruled that it is reversible error for jurors to be excluded from a petit jury because of their race.

There are more than a dozen reasons or causes on which a challenge for cause may be made. Without going through the whole list, they are of this nature: that his answers to the four questions asked by the court, or one of them, was not true; that he is a witness in the case; that he was on the grand jury that returned the indictment in this case; that he is insane; that he cannot read and write; that he has a serious hearing defect which makes him unfit for jury duty, etc.

When a venireman has been questioned by both sides, first by the state's attorney and then by the defendant's attorney, and he has not been disqualified and no peremptory challenge has been made against him, then he becomes a juror in the case. After all of the jurors have been selected, the judge will have the following oath administered:

> You solemnly swear that in the case of the State of Texas against the defendant, you will a true verdict render, according to the law and the evidence, so help you God.

The court may permit the jurors to separate and go to their own homes at night until the time the charge of the court is given to them. After that, they stay together until discharged, except for necessary separate sleeping quarters.

Following the jury selection, either side may request that the witnesses be placed "under the rule," which means that the witnesses must remain outside of the courtroom until they are called to the witness stand. This is to prevent them from hearing the testimony of the other witnesses, and in this instance the judge will instruct them not to talk among themselves or to others except the lawyers about matters pertaining to the case. Witnesses under the rule are attended by a court officer whose duty is to report to the court any violation of its instructions.

After the jury is seated in the jury box, the stage is set for dramatic clashes between opposing counsel. If the case is well-prepared by both sides, the state has, through its prosecutor and the law enforcement officers, combed carefully to find and have ready to present in court all of the evidence necessary to obtain a conviction of the defendant. They have their witnesses ready to give testimony intended to establish the facts alleged in the indictment against the defendant and bring about his conviction. This is in direct opposition with the defendant's attorney who has been equally diligent in finding every witness and having him ready to give testimony favorable to the defendant to prove him innocent of the indictment against him, for it may be the defendant's life that is at stake.

It should be kept in mind that the state's burden is to prove to the jury, who will be the judge of the facts, *beyond a reasonable doubt* that the defendant is guilty of the offense as charged. The circumstance of the offense may make this duty extremely difficult for the prosecuting attorney to discharge, though he may be absolutely sure in his own mind that the defendant is guilty. The prosecutor may make such a definite case against the defendant that the defendant's attorney is left with only one hope for his client and that is that he might create a *reasonable doubt* in the minds of the jurors. If he can accomplish only this, his client may walk out of the courtroom free.

The indictment is read to the jury by the prosecuting attorney.

The special pleas, if any, are read by the defendant's attorney, and a plea of "not guilty" is stated to the jury (if the defendant pleads not guilty, which is most often the case).

The prosecuting attorney tells the jury the nature of the accusation and the supporting facts.

The testimony on the part of the state is presented by calling on witnesses whose testimonies are expected to prove the charges against the defendant. Exhibits are introduced into evidence, such as any gun or knife that may have been used in committing the offense, written statements that may have been made by the defendant admitting the crime, and other things which the prosecuting attorney considers necessary to establish the guilt of the defendant. The defendant's attorney has the right to cross-examine each witness at the conclusion of his direct testimony.

During the presentation of the state's evidence, the defendant's attorney will be alert to object to any testimony, exhibits, or other evidence which he believes should not be presented, or any which he thinks he might have some chance to keep out. He does this by addressing the court stating that he objects to the testimony, and the grounds upon which he bases his objections, such as "it is hearsay," or "it is intended only to inflame the jury against this defendant," or other grounds.

The judge will rule on the objections by sustaining or overruling them as and when they are made. If he sustains an objection, the evidence is kept out. If he overrules the objection, then the question is to be answered or the offered exhibit is to be admitted. If the judge is in error in his rulings it may be grounds for reversal by the appellate court. The burden is on the defendant to call these errors to the court's attention as they are made so that the court will have an opportunity to correct them.

It is necessary that the defendant's attorney make a good record at the trial and show the particular errors of the court on which he will expect to reverse the case if it goes up on appeal. In the Court of Criminal Appeals, the objections cannot be raised for the first time.

After the state rests, the defendant's counsel states the defenses which the defendant relies upon and the facts expected to be proved in their support.

The testimony on the defendant's behalf is then presented. The defendant may testify but he does not have to do so. As the defense witnesses are examined by the defense counsel, the state's attorney will object to testimony he thinks should not be admitted, and the judge will rule on the objections as they are made by sustaining or overruling them.

For many years, appeals could be taken only by the defendant, not the state. Now, however, certain decisions of the trial court can be appealed by the state. It is a limited right, though. If the defendant is acquitted in the trial court, the state must be satisfied to set him free. If the defendant is convicted and given a lighter sentence than the state's attorney thinks he should have received, there is no appeal available to the state and the sentence stands.

This is a further example of how far our lawmakers have gone in protecting the accused; and it is based upon the premise that it is better to let the guilty go free than to punish the innocent. The state's attorney may cross-examine each defense witness at the conclusion of his direct testimony.

Rebutting testimony is offered by each side. The court can permit the introduction of further testimony at any time before the conclusion of the argument, if it considers that further testimony is necessary for justice.

After all the testimony, the judge starts preparing his charge to the jury. Before he gives it, each side is allowed a reasonable time to prepare, in writing, charges and instructions which they desire to be submitted to the jury. The judge will consider these and submit them, or alter them and submit them, or reject all or part of them as he chooses. The defendant's attorney will enter exceptions when necessary to make a good record for his client in the case. Finally, each side is given a copy of the charge to the jury before it is read to the jury, at which time the defendant's attorney will offer his final written objections to it.

The judge reads the charges to the jury, and in this, he gives them his instructions and tells them what the law is with respect to the case. Then he gives them a copy of the charges.

He must not comment on the weight of the evidence or give a summation of or comment on the credibility of the witnesses. The jury is the judge of the facts in the case, but it must accept the law as given by the court. The judge informs the jury of the penalty provided by law in case the accused is found guilty, but he does not instruct them to set the penalty. The jury's first function is to determine from the evidence presented in the trial and the law given them in the judge's charge whether the accused is "guilty" or "not guilty."

The attorneys in the case will offer their arguments after the charge has been read to the jury, and before they retire to consider a verdict. They, with the judge's consent, can arrange the order of argument as they choose, but the attorney for the state has the right to give the closing address.

The attorney on either side may object to the argument of the opposing attorney if he believes it to be improper, and the judge will immediately sustain or overrule the objection. If he sustains the objection, he often will instruct the jury to disregard that part of the argument which was objectionable. Each side, however, has the right of fair comment upon the evidence in the case and to make a summation of it for the jury. The prosecution tries to review it as putting the shadow of guilt upon the defendant and the defense tries to show his client to be innocent. Sometimes these arguments become impassioned and quite moving—sometimes they are overdone. But a well-reasoned and well-presented argument is helpful to the jury. The attorneys on both sides are officers of the court, but they present opposite viewpoints.

The jury retires to the jury room to consider its verdict at the conclusion of the arguments. They are kept together during their deliberations and are not permitted to talk to other people. They elect one of the members foreman in accordance with the judge's instructions. They may request to have in the jury room any written evidence and exhibits introduced in the case, and they may call on the judge for definitions of words in the charge, and sometimes for further instructions. The judge is generally reluctant to do much more than call their attention to the charge and instruct them to read it and to proceed with their deliberations, because he feels that the charge is complete in the first place and understandable by those qualified to serve on a jury in the second. He is mindful also of the record of reversible errors committed by judges who are too free with instructions to the jury.

The jury, if they can agree, will render a verdict, and they may find the defendant "not guilty" or "guilty as charged." If their verdict is "not guilty," the case is ended and the defendant is immediately released. If the verdict is "guilty," then comes the procedure for assessing the punishment. It may be that prior convictions for similar offenses will subject the defendant to more punishment than that for a single offense. In this case, evidence of prior convictions must be presented to the court by the prosecution, so the judge or the jury, whoever is to assess the punishment, may be properly informed.

If it is the jury who is to assess the punishment, the judge will give them a charge on the punishment informing them of the minimum and maximum penalties prescribed by law, and send them back to the jury room to complete the verdict by fixing the penalty. If the jury can agree on the amount of punishment, they return to the court with their verdict written out, and the foreman hands it to the court clerk. The judge calls the court to order and instructs the clerk to read the verdict. The judge then asks the jury if that is their verdict, and generally they indicate that it is. But if there is a dissent, one or more indicating that they did not understand it that way, the judge will send them back to the jury room for further deliberation. Finally, the verdict is complete, and the defendant's punishment is fixed.

At this point, the same as at the time when the jury brought in its verdict of "guilty," the attorney on either side may ask for a poll of the jury and his request will be granted. Then each juror is asked whether the verdict returned into court is his verdict. If all answer affirmatively, then their work is finished. If there is any dissent, they are sent back for further deliberation.

If the jury cannot agree on either the issue of guilt or punishment, it is commonly termed a *hung* jury, and they are discharged. This calls for a new trial at a later date.

If the defendant is found guilty and his punishment is assessed, the defendant's attorney almost always asks for a new trial. He has 30 days from the date sentence is pronounced in open court in which to file his motion with the court asking for a new trial. The court will grant a hearing on the motion and dispose of it by granting it or overruling it. There are nine different grounds on which the defendant's attorney may urge for a new trial. If the judge decides that reversible error has been made in the trial of the case, he will grant a new trial and the whole trial procedure must be gone through again. If the judge feels, however, the defendant has had a fair trial and that no valid grounds exist for a new trial, he will overrule the motion.

Generally, the defendant's attorney will give notice of appeal and take the case to the Court of Appeals. The Court of Appeals will hear the case *on the record,* which is a copy of the proceedings in the district court, the briefs filed by the attorneys on each side, and the arguments of the attorneys before the court. That court may affirm the judgment of the court below, or it may reverse that judgment and discharge the defendant, or it may reverse the judgment below and send the case back for a new trial. The case can then be appealed to the Court of Criminal Appeals, which is the "court of last resort" for criminal cases under Texas law. In some instances, an appeal may be carried to the United States Supreme Court on grounds that the defendant's rights under the United States Constitution have been violated.

Who Decides Punishment—Judge or Jury?

For the past several years, there has been confusion as to whether the judge or jury is to decide the punishment under the bifurcated procedure. The determination of punishment is made in a completely separate hearing, after the defendant has been found guilty. The intent of the 1965 legislation was to give the accused the choice of whether he wanted punishment assessed by the jury or by the judge.

Wording of the statute, though, made it unclear as to who would assess punishment in a capital case where the death penalty is asked by the state. In 1967 and 1973, the statute was amended. It now provides that it shall be the duty of the judge to assess the punishment unless (a) it is a case where the jury may recommend probation and the defendant filed his sworn motion for probation before the trial began, or (b) the defendant files in writing at the time he enters his plea his election have the jury assess punishment.

If a finding of guilty is returned, the defendant may, with the consent of the state's attorney, change his election. In potential death penalty cases, punishment must be assessed by the same jury that heard the case.

Conclusion

This is only an overview of basic procedure in criminal cases. Some people view procedures as mere technicalities. But nothing is as important to a free people as integrity in the procedures by which they can be convicted of crime. And though there is always room for improvement, the system works remarkably well day in and day out. For the most part, it protects us all from arbitrary and malevolent actions by those who exercise the power of government.

Index

About the Authors

Charles Turner, J. D., is currently an associate professor at Texas A&M University-Commerce. He was formerly the university attorney for East Texas State University, and has also served as president of the Texas Association of State University Attorneys.

The late **Ralph Walton, L. L. B.,** was past-president of Sparta Oil Company, and was a member of the Houston Bar Association, the State Bar of Texas, and the American Judicature Society.